Thomas A. Jaggar

The Man of the Ages

And other recent Sermons

Thomas A. Jaggar

The Man of the Ages
And other recent Sermons

ISBN/EAN: 9783337116927

Printed in Europe, USA, Canada, Australia, Japan

Cover: Foto ©ninafisch / pixelio.de

More available books at **www.hansebooks.com**

THE
MAN OF THE AGES
AND OTHER
RECENT SERMONS

BY THE
RT. REV. THOMAS A. JAGGAR, D. D.
BISHOP OF SOUTHERN OHIO

NEW YORK
JAMES POTT & CO. Publishers
FOURTH AVENUE AND 22D STREET
1898

Copyright, 1898, by
JAMES POTT & COMPANY.

TO
MR. AND MRS. FRANK HOUSTON WYETH
PHILADELPHIANS
FAITHFUL PARISHIONERS, LONG-LOVED FRIENDS
THIS VOLUME
IS GRATEFULLY DEDICATED

PUBLISHED BY REQUEST

CONTENTS.

I.	THE MAN OF THE AGES	1
II.	THE RECONCILING TRUTH	21
III.	GOD IMAGED IN HUMAN RELATIONSHIPS	41
IV.	CONTROL FROM WITHIN	61
V.	THE LOVE OF GOD IN CHRIST	77
VI.	LIFE IN THE LIGHT OF THE RESURRECTION	97
VII.	STAYING BY THE STUFF	117
VIII.	DOES GOD CARE?	139
IX.	THE TEMPLE OF GOD IN US	163
X.	THE TEMPLE AND THE STREET	181
XI.	THE WORTH OF MANHOOD	197
XII.	THE EVERLASTING POSSESSION	219
XIII.	"MY LORD AND MY GOD"	239
XIV.	OTHER MEN'S LABOURS	259
XV.	REALITY IN THE CHRISTIAN LIFE	277
XVI.	MORTALITY SWALLOWED UP OF LIFE: AN EASTER SERMON	297
XVII.	SEEKING FIRST THE KINGDOM OF GOD	315
XVIII.	CLEANSED IN GOING	335
XIX.	THE MILITARY IDEA	353
XX.	RELIGION AND SOCIAL SCIENCE	379

ID="1"

I.

The Man of the Ages.

I.

THE MAN OF THE AGES.

Jesus said unto them, Verily, verily, I say unto you, Before Abraham was, I am.—ST. JOHN viii. 58.

THERE is a confusion of tenses in this saying of Jesus Christ which strikes strangely upon the ear. It is language evidently from some sphere foreign to our earth. It seemed to the Jews awful blasphemy, for it was so that God had named Himself to Moses out of the burning, fiery bush on Horeb. Jesus Christ dared to rise, in His conflict with the baffled Pharisees, to this sublimity of presumption. There He stood, a care-worn peasant of Galilee, with nothing in the outward conditions of His life to separate Him from the humblest of His fellows. It was the claim of a lunatic, which could not have survived beyond the moment of its utterance, had there not been something in Him to give it dignity and conceivability. It has survived. It has stood the test of ages. "They crucified Him," but somehow it seems quite natural and not at all strange, as we read the words now, that He should have had to speak from outside of time—from the "eternal Now": "Before Abraham was, I am."

The words can mean nothing less than that He is "I AM" in and over all the ages of time. He claims to be unchangeably present—a living, undying force at every point of human history. It was a splendid claim. What, indeed, could realise more fully all that human need and philosophy and science are striving after than such a Man of the Ages, set like a fixed star in our firmament, and shining more and more, while other stars rise and set, or flash meteor-like across our view and vanish into darkness?

I ask you to think with me of some features of the Christ-life which seem to place Him above all other religious leaders and to confirm His claim to be the Man of the Ages.

I. And first note *that the ages which preceded Him were fulfilled in Him.* He came, not to destroy, but to fulfil. The word "fulfil" in the Greek of the New Testament means much more than our English word in its popular acceptation. It means to "fill up to the full," or, using the more philosophical form of expression, to "realise the full and complete ideal."

The teaching of Christ was not original,—it would have been a foreign tongue to the world of humanity if it had been,—but the truth of His person and life and work was original. It was the emerging into form and power and a new, visible creation, of that which had been struggling towards the light in the minds of men from the beginning. He was the "realised ideal" of that which they had been darkly groping after, "if haply they might find Him." He dimmed the lesser lights of Jewish, Egyptian, Persian, Buddhistic, and Greek thought.

It is not necessary to prove that all the ages of Jewish history were leading up to Him. This is a fact which is bound up in our Bible. He realised in Himself temple and prophecy. Christianity is the culmination and completion of that Judaism which reached back over twenty centuries. With the clear vision of one to whom and in whom all ages were living, He said to the Jews, in language from above, which they could not understand: " Your father Abraham rejoiced to see My day: and he saw it, and was glad."

Outside of the Jewish world were the nations of whom Christ said: " Many shall come from the east and the west, and sit down with Abraham, Isaac, and Jacob, in the kingdom of God." Confucius, Sakya-Muni the Buddha, and the Greek philosophers were prophets too, who saw as through a glass, darkly, the truth which Christ realised in fact. The Greek philosophy was the purest expression of spiritual thought, the loftiest reach of human reason, which the thinkers of the world had attained. But the beautiful abstractions of Plato, too remote for the common life of men, were transmuted by Christianity into the current gold of the very humanity that his mind regarded as hopelessly barbarian. Plato himself taught that " we must wait for one, be it a God or a God-inspired man, who will teach us our religious duties and take away the darkness from our eyes." The Christ in His person and life and word realised this long-looked-for ideal, and in the brightness of His rising made a new day for the world.

Renan has said: "Eliminate from the teaching of Jesus Christ all the moralities which were known to the world before Him, and what have you left?" It is a very shallow saying. No thoughtful Christian denies that there were moral instincts seeking and finding expression in the wisdom of philosophers before Christ. It is the worn-out taunt of sceptics that the golden rule is to be found in the teaching of Confucius. It is true that a negative form of it is to be found there: "Whatsoever ye would not that men should do to you, do ye not to them." The positive saying of Christ, "Whatsoever ye would that men should do to you, do ye even so to them," is a flowering out of it as superior as the law, "Thou shalt love thy neighbour as thyself," is superior to the Jewish negations, "Thou shalt not kill, steal, or commit adultery." There are doubtless many resemblances to be traced between the positive teaching of Christ and the fragmentary suggestions which preceded Him; but the fact remains that on these two commandments, in the broadest possible sense, hang all the law and the prophets: "Thou shalt love the Lord thy God with all thy heart, and . . . soul, and . . . mind, and . . . strength; and thy neighbour as thyself." Eliminate from the natural creation all the seething forces which were at work when "the earth was without form, and void; and darkness was upon the face of the deep," and what have you left? It is true that there would be no beautiful creation at all. But God said, "Let light be: and light was"; and man was evolved, made in God's image, after God's likeness.

The same is true in our spiritual world. The new creation in Christ Jesus, and its infinite possibilities, could have no existence apart from humanity and its strivings after God and truth; but "God," says Paul, "who commanded the light to shine out of darkness, hath shined in our hearts, to give the light of the knowledge of the glory of God in the face of Jesus Christ." The light and the life were potent in Him for a new creation, as they were not in all the chaotic ages which preceded Him. There was nothing in all the thought of the ages before Him worthy to survive which was not absorbed in the brightness of His shining as the sun absorbs the dawn.

II. But I ask you to observe again that, while the ages which preceded Christ were fulfilled, or filled full, by Him, *He overflowed the age into which He was historically born.* He was a Jew, but Judaism could not contain Him. His thought burst from the Mosaic seed-shell into words which were spirit and life. He had to speak *down* to the capacity of His own nation, as a teacher speaks to children by object-lessons. No one can read with an unbiassed mind the New Testament, and fail to be impressed by the immense reserve force of His character and words. He taught them "many things in parables" because they were in the childhood of the infinite life of that "whole family in heaven and earth" which was present to His mind. Even to His chosen few, unto whom it was "given to know the mysteries of the kingdom of God," He could not make Himself fully known. They began to realise the depth and universality of His purpose only after He had left the earth.

He was strangely outside of His own time; and yet He was no recluse, neither did He exhaust Himself in vague or wild speculations.

He was simply the carpenter's son, until He showed Himself in the broad daylight of those three brief years of public ministry. He was known then as the "Friend of publicans and sinners." His followers were poor, obscure, unlearned fishermen. He seems to have drawn them by the force of His personality rather than by His teaching. He touched the groaning humanity of His time with an infinite pity, which found expression in healing, helping acts, and which, reinforcing His words, marked the beginnings of a great uplifting. But His life was not understood. They said: "He casteth out devils through Beelzebub the prince of the devils." He preached the gospel to the poor, and proclaimed a kingdom not of this world. They looked for a temporal lord and kingdom.

He knew that His life and words, while He lived, could not be understood. This consciousness appears through all His living in time. It was the shadow of that cross which awaited Him at the end. He attempted no local or national reforms; He would not entangle Himself with any of the political, religious, or social questions of His time. They brought Him the tribute-money, asking if it was lawful to give tribute unto Cæsar or not, and He answered: "Render unto Cæsar the things that are Cæsar's; and unto God the things that are God's." They brought Him their marriage problems, and He replied to the question of divorce in words of profound meaning: "What God hath joined together, let not man put asunder"; and to the question, "Whose wife shall she be hereafter who has been seven times married?" "In the resurrection they neither marry, nor are given in marriage; but are as angels in heaven." One came to Him with a property grievance, saying: "Speak to my brother, that he divide the inheritance with me." He answered: "Man, who made me a judge and a divider over you? Take heed, and beware of covetousness." There is a sublime consciousness of something far greater than earthly empire—yes, higher than even we can yet understand—in His reply to Pilate when, haggard, bleeding, the crown of thorns upon His head, He stood before that wavering governor in the judgment-hall: "Thou sayest that I am a king. To this end was I born, and for this cause came I into the world, that I should bear witness unto the truth. Every one that is of the truth heareth My voice."

Because He could not possibly be understood by His own people, He had to die. It was strange, but true, that He could give His life and truth to the world only by dying. Had He yielded to the blind literalism of His own people, He might have been, like Mohammed, the maker of kingdoms, but He would not have been the world's Christ. He could not be the spiritual King of men, and take the sword. He could prove Himself superior only by yielding to the sword. He lived His life out to the bitter end with a calm, unfaltering purpose which no threatening could shake nor temptings of ambition cause to swerve. He gave Himself to the cross, and " He is alive for evermore."

III. I have said that the Christ fulfilled the past and overflowed the age in which He historically lived. There is another fact which adds to His years nineteen centuries. The present has not exhausted Him; He is still the "I AM."

That He once lived on the earth, and was

"crucified, dead, buried," the severest criticism will allow. That something happened after His death which gave a wonderful impulse to the faith and zeal of His disciples must also be admitted. That through and in them He has lived and been a powerful, wide-spreading influence down to the present (creating, indeed, a new civilization), are obvious, commonplace facts of history. Account as you may for the facts, there was such force in the leaven which Christ put into the minds of a few obscure men that it spread in spite of persecution, and permeated the known world. It is beyond all criticism true that His influence in the world has worked exactly as He said it would—"like leaven," silently, slowly, continuously, powerfully. It is a working, living force to-day, as perplexing to foes, and as inexhaustible in its meaning for mankind, as when He taught in Jerusalem. It is too late, in this age of long perspective down through the ages of history, to hold Jesus Christ responsible for the evil that has been done in His name. The very spirit of this later age which denounces it, is the evolution of His spirit through and over it. I am quite aware that in the fervent heat of our modern thought Christianity is being tested as never before. But through all the glow of the burning, fiery furnace, I see the glorified form of Jesus Christ shining with undimmed lustre. John Stuart Mill expressed the mind of pure, merciless, logical reason in the one concession which he was forced to make to revealed religion, in the words: "Whatever else may be taken away by rational criticism, Christ is still left, a unique figure, not more unlike all His precursors than all His followers; nor even now would it be easy even for an unbeliever to find a better translation of the rule of virtue from the abstract into the concrete, than to endeavor so to live that Christ would approve our life." The science of to-day recognises the infinities as it did not thirty years ago. The reconciliation of science with all honest progressive Christian thought is indeed a fact accomplished. There are boundless possibilities in this and other movements towards unity. I am quite sure that no unbiassed naturalist of thirty years ago would have recognised "the doctrine of Jesus Christ as the summit and crown of the organic series, . . . expressing the final result of that directed striving which began hundreds of millions of years ago, and through infinite toil and pain has led to this supreme accomplishment." It is the language of a mature naturalist of to-day who cannot be suspected of a religious bias. It is the clear, cold crystallisation of a mind working through the processes of long observation and experience, and as such is the type of a whole class of thinkers.

I well remember, in my own early ministry, the stir caused by Draper's somewhat virulent history of the "Conflict between Science and Religion." That history has been rewritten by a scholar of to-day, who discriminates, as Draper did not, between religion and dogmatic theology; and after an exhaustive, valuable, and severely impartial review of the latest biblical research, he uses these words: "It has disengaged more and more as the only valuable residuum,—like the mass of gold at the bottom of the crucible,—the personality, spirit, teaching, and ideals of the blessed Founder of Christianity."

Philosophy is imbued with the spirit of

Christ's teaching. The broadest thought along the lines of the theory of evolution finds the ultimate destiny of man in the time when the physical shall be dominated by the psychical, and in the truest sense "the kingdoms of this world shall become the kingdom of . . . Christ; and He shall reign for ever and ever," "King of kings, and Lord of lords." Literature is putting into popular form the story of the Christ, and both literature and art are full of Him in a renaissance of Christian thought peculiar to our time. A very modern French realistic painting suggests as the scene of the crucifixion a hill overlooking Paris, with the dead form and the weeping women, and a workingman shaking his fist over the gay, indifferent city.

Now do not suppose that I am blind to the fact that there is a wide-spread scepticism, or at least indifference to the forms of religion, in our time. I am not arguing that the world is Christian, but that Christ is working profoundly in the world's highest thought, and that He is surviving through the most intense criticism that can be focussed upon Him. It was through His own "preaching the gospel to the poor" that the new principle of free and universal education entered into our modern life. The world's best thought circulates through the whole body, and when that thought is reacting towards God and Christ and the infinities we need not dread the issue.

It means much, I think, for the average human nature of this year of grace that it is capable of responding to such fiction as Charles Dickens's " Christmas Carol." It is only in the warmth of that new spirit of humanity which Christ breathed into the world that we have become capable either of creating or of being touched by such a conception as that of the old miser weeping bitter, penitent tears over the vision of his own neglected grave, and crying out : " I will honour Christmas in my heart, and try to keep it all the year!"

I have said that Jesus Christ was the realised ideal of the ages which preceded Him; that He overflowed the age in which historically He lived ; and that, after nineteen centuries, He is before the world as fresh and inexhaustible as when He stood before the scornful Pilate. The doubt of the day finds itself more than ever perplexed by the question, What shall we do, then, with Jesus? As the past has not been able to exhaust Him, no prophet's vision is needed to perceive that *the future cannot outgrow Him.* "You may destroy our churches," said a French peasant to an atheist in the time of the French Revolution, "but you cannot destroy the stars which shine in the eternal heavens. The more you demolish our steeples, the more clearly shall we see these worlds above." The Star of Bethlehem abides, and must abide, because He contains within Himself principles which are eternal in the heavens. Humanity can never outgrow such truths as these: "God is a Spirit: and they that worship Him must worship Him in spirit and in truth." "Love God, and your neighbour as yourself." "Walk in the Spirit, and ye shall not fulfil the lust of the flesh." "This is life eternal, that they might know Thee, the only true God, and Jesus Christ, whom Thou hast sent." It matters little, so far as my present argument is concerned, whether He is regarded as the most consummate genius that the world ever knew, or as God manifest in the flesh; because the genius was so pure, far-seeing, and universal that there seems to be no rational escape from the conclusion that He was all that He claimed to be — Immanuel, God with us. I believe that the future will find in the fact of the Incarnation truth which shall reconcile the natural and the supernatural, and "gather together in one all things in Christ, both which are in heaven, and which are on earth."

Standing as we do upon the threshold of a new century, what thought could be more inspiring and helpful than this? As across the stormy sea, when the disciples were toiling in rowing, they saw Him walking upon the waters, and heard Him saying, "It is I; be not afraid," so may we be confident that He is above time and space, the master of wind and waves. There is no more certain good in this present scheme of things for you and me than to live as He would have us live — keeping under our bodies, and bringing them into subjection; subduing the flesh to the spirit; walking in love, as He also loved us, and gave Himself for us; seeking in every relation, as mothers, fathers, brothers, sisters, citizens, students, business men, and working-men, to make the world of our time the

better, purer, wiser, and happier for our being.
The great poet who has " crossed the bar " sang:

> "Ring out the old, ring in the new,
>   Ring, happy bells, across the snow:
>   The year is going, let him go;
>   Ring out the false, ring in the true."

He also sang:

> "Ring in the valiant man and free,
>   The larger heart, the kindlier hand;
>   Ring out the darkness of the land,
>   Ring in the Christ that is to be."

II.

The Reconciling Truth.

II.

THE RECONCILING TRUTH.

Jesus saith unto her, Woman, believe Me, the hour cometh, when ye shall neither in this mountain, nor yet at Jerusalem, worship the Father. Ye worship ye know not what: we know what we worship; for salvation is of the Jews. But the hour cometh, and now is, when the true worshippers shall worship the Father in spirit and in truth: for the Father seeketh such to worship Him.—St. John iv. 21–23.

THERE are few incidents of our Lord's life in which the human and the divine appear more beautifully blended than in this conversation with the Samaritan woman by Jacob's well. He was human in His weariness. Travel-worn, at the close of the day, He sat by the well. The woman came to draw water. He surprised her by asking her to give Him drink. She was surprised, because the Samaritans and Jews were political and religious foes. It was true at all times, and reaching to the smallest details of the ordinary daily life, that "the Jews have no dealings with the Samaritans." The divine life in Him escapes and overflows the prejudices natural to Him as a Jew. She exclaims, scornfully perhaps, "How is it that Thou, being a Jew, askest drink of me, who am a woman of Samaria?" He tells her, in language too spiritual for her comprehension, of the living water which He could give. She flippantly replies: "Sir, give me this water, that I thirst not, neither come hither to draw." She sees only a dusty, travel-worn Jew; but He speedily and sternly reads to her a page out of her own private life which startles her into reverence. "Go call thy husband, and come hither." "I have no husband," she replied. Jesus said: "Thou hast well said, I have no husband: for thou hast had five husbands; and he whom thou now hast is not thy husband: in that saidst thou truly." Convicted in her conscience, she seems confusedly to try to excuse herself by pleading the perplexities of the religious question of her time: "Our fathers worshipped in this mountain; and ye say, that in Jerusalem is the place where men ought to worship." It was human nature striving, as it has done in all ages,— not, perhaps, without reason,— to justify its immoralities by the disagreements and antagonisms of the religious.

Now observe how our Lord meets the problem in which her mind seemed to be entangled. He does not compromise with the Samaritan heresy, for He distinctly says: "Ye worship ye know not what: we know what we worship; for salvation is of the Jews." His people were in the truth so far as the historic question was concerned. They looked for the Messiah; they worshipped towards Him; and He was to come of the "seed of David according to the flesh." But He lifts the whole question out of the local and material into the light and air of a new spiritual day. He tells her that the worship of God is no longer to be limited to places, but that "the true worshippers shall worship the Father in spirit and in truth: for the Father seeketh such to worship Him." He brings in a larger, higher truth, which dissolves away the antagonisms which had their origin in partial knowledge, or ignorance of the whole truth. Neither Jew nor Samaritan had realised the true idea of worship.

They had localised God. They had thought of Him as outside of themselves. They had said, "Lo, here!" or "Lo, there!" and quarrelled. He said: "God is a Spirit: and they that worship Him must worship Him in spirit and in truth."

There are many timely suggestions for us in Christ's method with the Samaritan question. Here was the standing feud of ages, separating peoples whose religions had much in common, who lived in close neighbourhood, and yet neither had understood the real question involved. Their differences sprang from their ignorance of the entire truth. Had they understood that which Christ revealed, there would have been no ground for the long, bitter, angry war. The Jews were in the truth so far as it had progressed, and the Samaritans were essentially proselytes, deriving their doctrines and practices from Jewish sources, and regarded by the older tradition as on the level of ignorant Jews. The antagonism continued, and doubtless had its uses, until the hour came for the reconciling truth to disclose itself. There was a process of development going on, a secret, unseen growth, until the time was ripe for the dead branches to drop off or be pruned away, that the new life might have free course.

That which was true in the development of Judaism is true in the development of Christianity. There is "first the blade, then the ear, after that the full corn in the ear." The apostolic age, with its baptism of the Holy Ghost, did not exhaust or finally express the whole truth of Christ's teaching. As the words of patriarch and prophet contain deeper meanings than they knew, which a later age interpreted, so, too, the apostles, in their witness of the resurrection and its kindred doctrines, witnessed of mysteries which even they had not fully comprehended. St. Paul, with all his searching wisdom, exclaims, "Great is the *mystery* of godliness!" and it is the "*mystery* of the faith" which is to be "held in a pure conscience," that which he calls the "hidden wisdom." The same Holy Spirit which illumined the apostles is with the Church now, to realise through the faithful Christ's promise, "Lo, I am with you alway, even unto the end of the world." The word of Christ has deeper meanings than the honest seekers after truth have yet dreamed of. There is always some new treasure for the honest mind to find, some larger truth to appear when the time is ripe for it, some higher principle or definition to evolve itself and harmonise the lower and material antagonisms. It has a vitality which unfolds, as each age demands, new lights, new helps, new applications. I cannot help thinking that in the tendency now of all earnest thinkers to return to the simple creeds of the first age, the creeds which enshrine the simple divine facts of Christ's life, we have the most cheering sign of growth, of giving way to the richer life, the fresher meanings which are coming—the springtime of a better, broader, sunnier day. Was not St. Paul thinking forward to such times of riper, broader knowledge when, magnifying the riches of God's grace, he declares this to be the divine purpose, " that in the dispensation of the fulness of times He might gather together in one all things in Christ, both which are in heaven, and which are on earth; even in Him"? Here is the very suggestion of that unity towards which the scientific, the social, and the religious thought of the age is tending.

The Christian Church has been slow to realise that there must be unsettlings and changes and new definitions in the progress of a living truth. The Church has walked with Christ like the disciples on the way to Emmaus, whose "eyes were holden that they should not know Him." They were sad and hopeless because the tomb had been found empty, and they could not solve the mystery of the missing body of their Lord. They had not understood the full meaning of that divine life and the power of His resurrection. "O foolish men," He exclaims, "and slow of heart to believe all that the prophets have spoken!" The larger, spiritual meaning of His life dawned upon them as He interpreted to them the Scriptures, and in the breaking of bread they knew Him. The story of the Church in its movement down through the ages has been like that. Minds have been holden so that the full meaning of His life from the dead has been only partially perceived. He has been looked for in the tomb rather than in the open day; and yet many hearts have burned within them, not knowing Him as He spake with them by the way. God had His own wise purpose in keeping back the liberation of the mind until the hour came. The hour came when the art of printing made it possible for the spirit and truth to loose minds from the wintry bondage of ecclesiastical despotism. That wintry time conserved principles and warmed into life a learning which burst the icy fetters when the time was ripe. The progress of Christianity, as it strove with the ignorance and earthliness of men, necessarily created antagonisms. They were like the mists which writhed and tossed upon the earth when God said, "Let there be light: and there was light." There were spectres of heresy and error which in the dim light seemed to be monstrous shapes, but which were dissolved away under the advancing day. It is the glory of this age of free and daring thought that Christianity is open to investigation, its pure springs uncovered, barriers of prejudice broken down, and truth searched for with a clearer vision than ever before.

The definite thought towards which I have been travelling through these very general suggestions is that the attitude of the Christian, in our day of free and much earnest thought, should be that of looking always for the higher, broader truth which may reconcile antagonisms. In this elder age, with nineteen centuries of history behind us, it should not be possible for the hating antagonism which marked the difference between the Jew and the Samaritan to repeat itself. I am not thinking only of the differences which separate the various religious bodies within the Church of Christ. They are practically inconvenient; they seem to create much friction and waste; but they are not serious. In the moral as in the physical world diversity of form is the natural and necessary expression of exuberance of life. The incoming of a larger sense and realisation of that spiritual brotherhood which is the fundamental order of Christ's appointment is already beginning to submerge our minor differences and lift us up to a better understanding. I am thinking of the differences between the Christian and all honest thinkers who are moving towards God through nature, through other religious systems, or through the unseen mysteries of the spirit itself.

As Christians we hold to the truth, as the *truth is in Jesus*. This is our faith in which we stand, our "anchor of the soul, both sure and steadfast, and which entereth into that within the veil." There can be no weak compromising, if we are really rooted and grounded in Christ, with that which actually contradicts this truth. But the truth in Him, in His divine person and word, must necessarily be in harmony with all other truth everywhere; otherwise it is not God's truth. No sound has yet reached us out of the realms of absolute truth which proves the hidden wisdom of Christ to be a false note among the eternal harmonies,—an errant discord. Science itself in some of its best thinkers sees in the doctrine of Christ the "summit and crown of a series of organic developments." The habit of looking always for the harmonising element among all the discords of opposing sects, systems, and philosophies lifts us above the entanglements of mere prejudice, and makes us receptive towards the larger truth when it comes. We are helping, not obstructing, if our minds are in the great movement towards God. The differences which exist among all seekers after God, whether within or without the Church of Christ, have their origin in this fact: "We know in part: but when that which is perfect is come, then that which is in part shall be done away." No one can study the New Testament and fail to perceive that there are meanings within meanings. Our Lord certainly looked far on through a long vista of hazy distances when He said to His disciples: "I have yet many things to say unto you, but ye cannot bear them now. Howbeit when He, the Spirit of truth, is come, He shall guide you into all the truth." If this be so, why should we not be living and thinking always with our faces towards the dawn, always listening for the voice which shall say: "Neither in this mountain, nor yet at Jerusalem, shall men worship the Father. . . . But . . . the true worshippers shall worship Him in spirit and in truth"?

When the disciples returned from the village where they had been to buy food, they marvelled that He was speaking with a woman. It was not only unusual for a Jewish rabbi to talk to a woman, but in this case there was an added shock to their prejudices in the fact that she was a Samaritan woman. It was a shock kindred to that which a mind intrenched in its own beliefs experiences, when the more daring Christian thinker, escaping from his prejudices, looks fairly at other systems than his own, and considers what of truth or good there may be in them, or how they may be brought into unity with the larger truth which he holds. Christ had nothing to learn from the woman, but He did not antagonise. He found soil ready and less encumbered with pharisaic and traditional prejudices than among His own people. He was conscious of a harmony in the true spiritual idea of worship, and led her mind up to it. Paul followed his Lord's example. When preaching to the Athenians he did not denounce their idolatry, though his spirit was provoked within him as he beheld the city full of idols. He took for his text the inscription upon one of their altars, "To an unknown God," and declared: "What, therefore, ye worship in ignorance, this set I forth unto you."

If any one supposes that such an attitude as this is only a convenient way of accommodating ourselves to views which undermine our own belief, let him look at Christ's words to the Samaritan woman, and let him find their ultimate limitation if he can: "God is a Spirit: and they that worship Him must worship Him in spirit and in truth"; "for the Father seeketh such to worship Him." I only point to the words as the climax of the whole subject, not attempting an exposition of them. Think what infinite possibilities of spiritual experience lie between these two ideas—the worshipper seeking Him in spirit, and the Father seeking the worshipping spirit. Think what truth inclusive of all conceivable spiritual development is here. Let the restless minds of men search the old Bibles and the new as they may,—let them come from the East and the West, and the North and the South, eager voyagers upon an unknown sea, looking for the "land which is very far off,"—I trust the Christ still. He opens boundless horizons before me. My fellow-voyagers can show me no diviner possibilities than are enclosed within His promise. When I was a young man fresh from the seminary I thought that I had almost exhausted the meaning of these words of Christ when I showed their application to the worship of our lips in public and in private. I gathered a few drops in the palm of my hand, and fancied I had emptied the ocean. Now I see that there are infinite depths of meaning in them, reaching to the remotest possibilities of the everlasting life beyond time. "God is Spirit," and in spirit—that is, in our spirits—we must worship Him. Truth is the way that leads to Him. In spirit by way of truth we look for Him wherever He may reveal Himself. Nature leads us far on into the truth of God. We follow gladly, and rejoice with the reverent student in the ever-widening vistas which are opening into the unknown. Where the naturalist can no longer find his way, we take the hand of Christ, and looking into His face, see the light of the knowledge of the glory of God there. While we are in the flesh we cannot understand God otherwise than through the conditions and limitations of the flesh; but we are not to rest in the flesh, or in nature, or mere form, or anything outside of us. The Samaritan woman did not appreciate His lofty words; she only answered humbly: "I know that Messias cometh: when He is come, He will tell us all things." Jesus replied: "I that speak unto thee am He." He was the guide by whom might be reached those distant heights which seemed to her so far up in the clouds. We know Him no more after the flesh, but He gives us in spirit a new and definite conception of God. He is the Word, expressing or interpreting God to us. The idea of personality in God which Christ gives does not limit; it only saves us from indefiniteness. That personality is Fatherhood. This is a figure of speech drawn from our human relations. We could not understand love in God, or feel it near to our spirits, otherwise than through the human forms in which it is feebly shadowed forth. The limitation of love is in these, but through them we may rise to the largest possible conception of love as a spiritual reality in the relation of God to our spirits. The Jews were taught the unity and holiness of God by forms suited to the childhood of the race. He was veiled within the holy of holies, and approached only through sacrifice and priest and high priest. In Christ He comes near as the Father, seeking the spirit to draw it out in a spiritual and universal worship. Our spirits must needs think of God and realise Him in word-forms, which are the best possible until word-forms yield to the developments of a higher state of being, and we no longer see "through a glass, darkly," but "face to face."

Why, then, should we not trust Christ for all that He reveals to us of God, and let the Father of our spirits, seeking the true worshippers, find us—find us in our spirits? Why should we not look for Him, where only He can be known in His fulness, within the temple of our body, in the sanctuary of our being, the place where the real self hides away and weeps, perhaps, over the good that it would and does not, and the evil that it would not and yet does? Keeping ourselves under the guidance of the divine Spirit, who is made known to us through Christ, we may live superior to the changes and unsettlings of the present. Deep shadows may rest upon the valleys, and mists veil the distant mountain-tops; but we shall be conscious of the larger light which is over all, and shall be able to reconcile the mists and the shadows with the coming day. In our first feeble vision of Christ we are like the blind men to whom He restored sight. They saw men as trees walking. There are minds which never grow out of such feebleness of vision. They are fixed in their first impressions. They will not see beyond that which in education or otherwise they have received. If others insist and the opinion spreads widely that men are not trees walking, their world is out of order; all seems lost. The growing vision, always keeping itself in the light of Christ, sees that the confused forms of moving thought are men advancing into the light, working towards a unity which shall be revealed in the fulness of time. St. Paul saw the unfolding cycles of our destiny widening ever towards a spiritual consummation, in that chapter of the resurrection which we read over our dead, where his thought travels on from Christ the first-fruits to those who are Christ's at His coming; and "then cometh the end, when He shall have delivered up the kingdom to God, even the Father"; and then "shall the Son also Himself be subject unto Him that put all things under Him, that God may be all in all."

III.

God Imaged in Human Relationships.

III.

GOD IMAGED IN HUMAN RELATIONSHIPS.

If ye then, being evil, know how to give good gifts unto your children, how much more shall your Father which is in heaven give good things to them that ask Him?—St. Matthew vii. 11.

I THINK life would be very different to us if we could give vivid reality in our minds to the term "Father" as applied to God. Do we not commonly think of it as a figure of speech, pleasant in its suggestions, but a mere accommodation, after all, to our human weakness? It is a generic term including motherhood and the mother heart, and indeed all the pure affections which enter into the parental relations. These affections are, as we all know, the purest elements in our present life. They make the bitter waters sweet. They constitute the family and the home. No words are needed to tell what they are, or what the world would be without them. That distinguished senator who for long years, it is said, carried close to his heart a little shoe, the memento of a dead child, knew what a father's love is. His heart beat with a broader sympathy, a nobler impulse, and a diviner purpose because he knew it and kept it ever living within him. That mother who was found frozen to death in the deep snow of a Scotch glen, with her living child clasped to her breast and wrapped in the shawl which she had stripped from her own perishing body, knew what a mother's love is, and so did the child when it was old enough to think, and feel the desolation of its loss. There is nothing in all the Old Testament literature more touching than those words from God in the prophecy of Isaiah: "As one whom his mother comforteth, so will I comfort you"; and that was a touch of nature which keeps ever fresh the parable of the prodigal son, when, feeding with the swine, "he began to be in want," and said, "I will arise and go to my father."

Yes, the prodigal turned back from his folly to the father and the father's house. How slow we are to realise the splendour of the truth contained in the old familiar story! When we "begin to be in want," when there is no more a father or mother to rest upon, when we stand, as we must sooner or later, alone in the universe, children gone from us, bereaved in our affections and sympathies, realising the inconstancy of the present and shrinking from the chill mystery of death, then we say within ourselves: "God cannot feel towards us as we have felt towards our children, nor may we dare to feel towards Him as our children have felt towards us. No; He is Spirit—far above us, infinitely foreign to our sphere. How can we presume to think that He is anything like father or mother as we may have known them in this world!"

Why not? I ask. The father and mother love is imperfect, being limited by sin and ignorance; therefore our Lord says: "If ye, being evil, know how to give good gifts unto your children, how much more your Father which is in heaven!" He reasons up from the discriminating love of the earthly parent to God. This is the strong underlying thought which seems to me so wonderfully suggestive. He does not use the human fatherhood as a mere figure to illustrate something which may possibly exist in God towards us, but which may be something very different and far removed from the reality which is so precious to us here. He is not using figures of speech; He is arguing. His argument is that if the earthly father knows how to give good gifts unto his children, how much more the heavenly Father! The earthly is to Him the feeble, imperfect type of which the great original is in God. If ye know the father and the mother love, how much more God, whose image ye but feebly reflect, and from whom, as your Creator, that very love is derived! The human fatherhood is not, therefore, something more than we may ever really dare to think of as in God, but something infinitely less than the reality which is in Him.

I suppose that even the most superficial readers know what distant flights our science has made within a few years by the aid of spectrum analysis. Reasoning up and out across millions of miles of space from that rainbow-hued image of light which the prism forms, and which is known as the spectrum, men have learned that the sun and remoter worlds are akin to our earth. Not many years ago all that could be known of the nature of the bodies that shine in our firmament was conjecture. Now we know by the spectrum that the elements we are familiar with here, exist in them. There is a direct relation between the prismatic colours which the earth elements give and the sun shining in his strength ninety-three millions of miles distant from us. That sun is no longer to be thought of as something different from our earth and inconceivably foreign to it in its substance. The same matter which we know in its grosser forms here, glows in a state of fiery, vaporous energy there.

It may be said, using this comparison, that the human fatherhood is the spectrum of God. He is Father, not in the material sense, but in the far broader and intenser spiritual sense of which the material form is only the " outward and visible sign." " How little," say we, in our blind ignorance, " can He who is so remote from us understand our feelings!" "*How much more,*" said our Lord Jesus Christ, reasoning up from the broken lights of our human state to the infinite Father.

If there could be any doubt that this was our Lord's thought, His own life would dispel it; for was it not in the consciousness of Sonship towards God that He lived, taught, suffered, and died? Was it not the peculiar beauty of His perfect manhood that the Father was always real to Him? The reality was dawning upon Him when, standing in the midst of the doctors, He said to His mother, who sought Him sorrowing: "Wist ye not that I must be about my Father's business?" It came upon Him in all the fulness of its power when that voice broke from the clouds at His baptism, saying: "This is my beloved Son, in whom I am well pleased." It appears in the strong, brave words with which He met His hating opposers: "He that sent me is with me: the Father hath not left me alone; for I do always those things that please Him." "I and the Father are one." It was comfort and strength to Him in every hour of trial, and when the disciples forsook Him and fled this was His consolation: "I am not alone, because the Father is with me." The reality was so strong and controlling in Him that all other relations were subordinate to it. When they told Him that His mother and His brethren stood without, He stretched forth His hand towards His disciples, and said: " Behold, my mother and my brethren! For whosoever shall do the will of my Father which is in heaven, he is my brother, and sister, and mother." What a lesson this for us who live our pitiful, contracted, selfish lives within the circle of mere natural affections, when we should be living out through them into the larger and eternal sympathies of the whole family of God! We follow Him down into the valley of the shadow of death, and through all the gloom and agony we hear the same note sounding: " Father, . . . not as I will, but as Thou wilt." " Father, forgive them." And then the last sigh, breathing the words, " Father, into Thy hands I commend my spirit."

It may, however, be said that Christ realised a Sonship towards God which we may not claim, because He was essentially divine. It is true that words are used to express His relation to the Father in the mysterious triunity of the

Godhead, which mean something infinitely beyond our understanding. He was "the only begotten of the Father, full of grace and truth." "No man hath seen God at any time; the only begotten Son, which is in the bosom of the Father, He hath declared Him." "No man hath ascended up to heaven, but He that came down from heaven, even the Son of man which is in heaven." Here we have language which evidently labours to manifest in time, and in terms of the human relation of father and son, sublime mysteries of a supernatural sphere. He has come down from heaven, and is in heaven. He is the Son of God moving in time, and yet is in the bosom of the Father. He speaks out of that eternal "Now" which cannot be expressed in time except by a confusion of tenses which is strange to us.

But the fact remains that He does choose the relation of Father and Son to express His own relation to the unseen God. There is something in that relation, therefore, which is the type of the mystery veiled in the Godhead. He draws our minds up from it to the glory which He had with the Father (always the

Father) before the world was. When, therefore, He tells us to take this same human relation, and think up from it to the "how much more" of Fatherhood in God towards us, He certainly means that the sense of God as our heavenly Father should be as intensely real to us as it was to Him.

It was, indeed, for the very purpose of warming into life this dormant sensibility, and bringing us back into the reality of a lost sonship, that He took upon Him our nature and was made in the likeness of men. Paul defines the gospel in one brief but exhaustive sentence: "God was in Christ, reconciling the world unto Himself." In Christ God reconciles Himself unto the world through the perfect obedience of His Son even unto death; and the world is reconciled unto God because in Christ He may be known as really the "Father of our spirits," the Lord God, "full of compassion, and gracious, slow to anger, and plenteous in mercy and truth, keeping mercy for thousands, forgiving iniquity and transgression and sin, and that will by no means clear the guilty."

The world needed reconciling; for the world,

through a sense of sin and the ills that sin had brought with it, nursed hard thoughts of God. We all of us, in our world of to-day, need reconciling; for the face of things as we see it is stern and even cruel. Conditions and circumstances environ us which often seem to contradict the thought of any love outside of the perishing relations in which we stand. God in Christ reconciles, because one long look of faith at Him shows that a man may be a son of God in all the attributes which we may justly look for in one claiming to be that, and yet suffer even to the shame of the cross and the cry in the darkness, "My God, my God, why hast Thou forsaken me?" That He should have consented to suffer, permitting evil to spend itself upon Him in order that we might be brought back to the realisation of God as our Father, is the truth which must touch our hearts and consciences as no other manifestation possibly could. This is the real meaning of His life for us. It could not have touched us had He been exempt from the pains which oppress us. He was made our perfect Saviour through suffering. He was "declared," said Paul, "to be the Son of God with power, . . . by the resurrection from the dead." The supreme credential of His claim to be our Redeemer, and the supreme fact which makes Him potent to win human hearts, is the triumph through and over sin, the cross, and the grave.

Now if it is possible for us, through faith in Jesus Christ, to be born anew into a realisation of sonship with God, our human relations appear in quite new lights; our point of view is changed. Love and life are as essentially wedded in our human experience as light and warmth. Deride as we may the sentimentalities of poet and romancer, love moves the world as truly as the sun is the source of every form of energy on the earth. We have striking evidence in the novels which flood society, and for which there seems to be a more unquenchable thirst than for any other kind of literature. But the forms of love which youth idealises, which marriage sanctifies, which are beautiful in motherhood, and the springs of purest joy in the relation of brother and sister, and friend with friend, are fading forms at best. Our habit is to rest in them as the only fountains which can satisfy our thirst. The springs dry up. The ideals shrivel into very weak, homely flesh and blood. The inevitable death breaks up the forms, and we are not satisfied. We are like children who see only the pretty colours of the spectrum, and nothing of the worlds beyond which they interpret. The man who thinks, translates the prismatic hues and proves the kinship of his earth with other worlds and with the blazing sun which his eyes unshielded cannot look upon.

It is from this earthly habit of seeing only the form, that Christ by His manifestation of God the Father would redeem us. This is the meaning of words which may have seemed harsh to you: "If any man come to me, and hate not his father, and mother, and wife, and children, and brethren, and sisters, yea, and his own life also, he cannot be my disciple." He does not, of course, mean hate in the personal, malignant sense which we associate with the word. His own example and the whole spirit of His life and teaching forbid the thought. He uses an intense word to make strong by contrast the ardour of the love which we owe to Him, the manifested God. He deepens the shadow, as the artist does, to bring out and make vivid the high lights. He simply means that which He expressly states in another place: "He that loveth father or mother more than me is not worthy of me." But I prefer the intenser form of the saying, because it makes so vivid the claims of the higher love. There is always an element of hate in fervent love. Jealousy is the form it takes. "The Lord our God is a jealous God," and therefore commands, "Thou shalt have none other gods beside me." Jealousy is the shadow of love. The fervency of the love is measured by the depth of the shadow. Christ taught that a man shall leave his father and mother and cleave unto his wife. Here is the same thought on the earthly plane. Carry it up to the Father of our spirits who is seeking us through all the earth-forms, and the meaning is that there shall be in us such an ardour of love towards Him kindled by the sense of His love for us that we shall be jealous of every human relation which would keep us back from the obedience which His love in us compels. I have been reading the wonderful story of Nansen's three years in the arctic ice. He left the wife and child to whom he was devoted, and risked his life in that daring journey. He did not love his wife less because the ambition to know drove him out into that perilous polar waste. He brought back to her a fame in which she too is lifted up and immortalised. We do not love in our human relations less because we rise through them into the faith of God's love in Jesus Christ. We only bring back to them immortality.

Men are constantly sacrificing their affections to gratify a passion for adventure or the desire for fame. Shall it be counted strange that a man, in seeking to know God, should have to renounce every earthly tie which might restrain him? Our human relations are glorified in the light of that knowledge. We see them no longer as ends of being, but as buds cradling within themselves the promise of a larger life to come. We love wisely, because we see that the breaking of the bud must precede the blooming of the flower. We love purely, because no gross love can survive in the upper atmosphere of a spiritual mind. All our affections are intensified and purified because lifted up into

God, where every pure love shares in the "how much more" of His love as compared with the evil and the littleness of our earthly relations.

I cannot conclude without calling your attention to the idea of discrimination which we find in our Lord's words: "If ye, being evil, know how to give good gifts unto your children" (that is, know how to discriminate), "how much more your Father in heaven?" Do we not have to train our children, by the very compulsion of our love, in the way of the cross? Do we not have to deny them much that they would like because our mature experience knows what is best for them? Children's trials in small matters are very real and cost them many tears. We children of a larger growth, if we would be the children of our Father which is in heaven, must on every rational ground expect a like discipline. We are all prodigal sons, wandering in a far country, until we turn from the riotous living and the husks and the swine, and seek pardon in the Father's house. Do not, however, suppose for a moment that the Father's love will or can do you any good while you continue wilfully in riotous living or in that lower degree of vice, feeding with the husks and the swine. You must give up your own way and come into His way of repentance, and faith in the Lord Jesus Christ, and the righteousness of a spiritual mind which comes by faith, or you can have no part in the endless joy of the Father's house. "As many as are led by the Spirit of God, they are the sons of God." His love is not an indulgent smile of complacency towards everything and everybody. It is a righteous love, and will " by no means clear the guilty." To be led by the Spirit while we are in the flesh, and in a world which constantly appeals to the flesh, means taking up the cross daily.

A certain French reformer invented a new religion which he wished to impose upon his country. He called it theophilanthropy. In spite of his passionate endeavours he made but little progress, and sought the advice of Talleyrand. "I am not surprised," said the shrewd statesman, "at the difficulty you experience. It is no easy matter to introduce a new religion. But I will tell you what I recommend you to do. I recommend you to be crucified, and to rise again on the third day." There was deeper meaning, perhaps, than he thought in his flippant words. No religion can lift us to God our Father out of this present sensual, selfish world which does not involve a being crucified and rising again. Paul expressed the same thought when he wrote: "Therefore we are buried with Him by baptism into death: that like as Christ was raised up from the dead by the glory of the Father, even so we also should walk in newness of life." If we fuse away all the accretions of a dogmatic theology from these words we find that they contain simply the experience and faith of the child. He is denied something which seems very good to him. He wipes away his tears, and, submitting to the father's or the mother's will, rises to the better life which their love ordains for him.

I have only suggested truths which hours and volumes could not exhaust. I hope you have caught something which may help you. I have tried to show that, as the scientist dares to reason out from his spectrum to worlds in space and to the sun itself, so we may dare to reason up from our dearest human relations to the "how much more" of "our Father which is in heaven."

Have you been living in sin, and do you feel the deep, unsatisfied need of a soul that has been feeding on husks? Give effect to the prodigal's resolve, and arise and go to your Father. Are you sorrowful, alone, friends gone or seemingly faithless, old age closing round you, and death near? Oh, if your heart is only in its purpose true to God, with what comfort may you rest in Him and feel, with Christ, "I am not alone, for the Father is with me"! And when death comes, as come it must to every one of us, what shall be our refuge if it be not in the Father of our spirits? If there is any cloud between Him and your spirit, it is an earth-born cloud, which may, in the faith of His forgiving love through a reconciling Saviour, condense into showers of fertilising repentance, and leave a clear sunset sky for the perfect repose of a last hour. "Father, into Thy hands I commend my spirit."

IV.

Control from Within.

IV.

CONTROL FROM WITHIN.

Casting down imaginations, and every high thing that is exalted against the knowledge of God, and bringing every thought into captivity to the obedience of Christ.—2 COR. X. 5.

I CAN imagine a condition of being in which spirits might know one another at once, without the interposition of bodies or the imperfect medium of language. We are really, even the closest friends, very far apart in this world. There is something sad in the eager way we look into one another's faces and listen to one another's words in the effort to become acquainted. The real life of every one of us is lived in the silence of his thoughts— thoughts which control him, it may be, but which never find expression in words; thoughts which he hides because they might not be understood, or masks under fair words and a correct deportment because he would blush to have them known.

Now it seems to me that Christianity is very true at least in this, that it aims to take hold of the hidden life in which we really live, the life of our thoughts, and so to control us from within, "bringing every thought into captivity to the obedience of Christ."

I ask you to consider with me the relation of this principle of control from within to the three necessary elements of a true manhood or womanhood: *overcoming—being—knowing.*

Overcoming is the first and constant necessity which is forced upon us when we try to lead a noble life. Temptation must be overcome and sin cleared away. It is almost impossible, say some, to live up to the Christian standard of right under the pressure of competition in business, or to exercise self-control in view of the scenes and sounds which appeal to appetite, ambition, and self-interest. I grant that it means a fight to keep pure in the midst of an ungodly world; but do you know that it is scarcely less difficult to live a pure life apart from an ungodly world? The seclusion of a hermit's cell is no protection against temptation if a man be temptable, because his real world of temptation is that which he conjures up out of the thoughts and imaginations of his own heart. The power of the pleasures, profits, and prizes of life to seduce into sin does not reside so much in them as in that which they find in us. The man who yields to licentiousness, to dishonest practices for the sake of getting rich, or to maxims, opinions, or parties which are opposed to his honest convictions for the sake of place or popularity, has prepared himself to yield. The debasing habit, act, pursuit, or whatever it may be, was entertained in thought before it took form in outward fact. Such is the invariable course of the yielding and sinking of a man's moral nature until he is completely under the dominion of the world, the flesh, and the devil. He familiarises himself with the thought of sin. The thought becomes an imagination in which he revels long before he would deem himself capable of a corresponding act. Opportunity comes, and there is no power of resistance. The forces without gain an easy victory because the fortress is full of traitors within. If you consider carefully the workings of your own heart, you will see that the temptations which appeal to your senses begin to get power over you when you give thought to them. Here, then, the battle with sin must begin. It is comparatively easy to overcome if you meet and exterminate temptation in its first suggestions. It will not get into you. It will have no chance to gain a hearing. The conscience, like a polished mirror, will be kept so sensitive that the least breathing of that which is bad will betray itself. The men who talk, as some do nowadays, about the impossibility of self-control, the necessity of a certain amount of license, and allowance for varieties of temperament and circumstance, assume that the strength of temptation is altogether in that which appeals to us from the outside. They overlook entirely the fact that they would not be liable to be set on fire by it if they did not habitually store up inflammable material within themselves. In fact, we often create our own temptations by putting ourselves in the way of scenes and persons and books which will gratify cherished desires. We live so powerfully in the imagination of certain events which might be that we try in ways that we will not admit to ourselves to bring them around to us. We slyly encourage opportunities, and then, when we have fallen into temptation, make ourselves believe that we have been the victims of circumstance. Once tamper with the thought, and begin to parley with it and then to justify that which it proposes to you, and you are lost. The door is open, and the whole dark train of imaginings and self-deceits and passions and evil-doings is pressing in behind.

"Keep thy heart," therefore, "with all diligence; for out of it are the issues of life." It is a garden in which may be made to grow, under the sunny influence of Christ's love and grace, plants which would make your whole life fragrant and beautiful and fruitful in blessing to the world; but if we suffer thoughts which defile to take root, there is no hope for our garden. They are weeds which are certain to overrun and destroy. It is not enough to keep them down out of sight. They must not be allowed to germinate. The soil must be kept clear of them. To cut off their flowering on the surface simply strengthens and makes them more deadly underneath. They will certainly take possession and grow rank and uncontrollable if we do not keep them rooted out.

But there is something more than overcoming sin or not doing wrong. That is only the negative side of a true life. See how the principle of bringing every thought into captivity is related to our second point—*being*. Being is character. Character is that which a man really is in the complexion and fibre of his being, and not merely that which he seems to be. How are we to attain or form soundness of being, so that men may trust us and our personality be solid oak in the social structure? It is commonly supposed that if a man aims to conform himself strictly to the received standards of right, and makes it his habit to be just and true in all his dealings and faithful to his promises, he will be such a character. I should say that he might seem to be, but the reality of that seeming would depend upon something more than his words and actions. How often has it happened that men trusted in a community, and rooted firmly in the respect and confidence of all who knew them, have suddenly fallen with a crash, as we have heard great forest-trees fall in the calm night! The world thought that they were men of sound character; they seemed to be secure in their pride of place; but they fell as the old tree of the forest falls—because it is corrupt at the core. While they were forming around themselves a reputation for integrity, they were not taking care of their thoughts. They had rules for their words and actions, but they had no law for their minds.

The language of St. Paul is very suggestive. It implies that the thoughts are habitually lawless and impatient of control. They must be taken prisoners by force of will and compelled (as the original has it) into a "listening submission to Christ." Every man who has any regard for his interest and reputation takes care of his words and actions, but few think of attempting to control the wild rioting within them. Yet here alone can the conquest be made for character, and a foundation be laid which shall make the whole building secure and able to survive even the shock of the judgment-day. I cannot imagine how any rule could be more thorough, and potent to control, than that which made St. Paul the brave, pure man he was, and which he calls "the obedience of Christ." Whatever you may think intellectually about Jesus Christ, you know that in the presence of the very thought of Him impurity, deceit, hate, and selfishness shrink like creatures of the night before the dawn. A mind surrendered to His obedience is a mind surrendered to purity, truth, and love. The character which in loyalty to such a Master repels every thought which is at war with these, necessarily purifies itself. Suppose you made it your practice never to do or say anything which you would blush to have your mother or sister or dearest friend see or hear. Your life would be tolerably correct outwardly. But suppose you went further, and made it the rule of your life never to entertain a thought which you would be ashamed to have them know. Do you not see how such a rule would work to keep your life pure at its fountain? Ah, we know that under the pleasing manners which many a young man assumes in the presence of pure women there is a brood of vile thoughts and imaginations. The man is a sham—a whited sepulchre. If the restraints which he puts upon his behaviour were carried into his thoughts, if he felt that the pure eyes were upon him there, he would begin to know what purity is. Now put the Lord Jesus Christ in the place of mother or sister or friend, and you have the Christian rule. He asks you to put aside your reasonings and pride and prejudices, and every high thing which exalts itself against the knowledge of God, and let Him rule in your heart. He asks you to make it your habit to bring every thought to the test of His purity, truth, and love. He asks you to let the lightning of His indignation be felt against every evil suggestion and foul imagination. He asks you to honour your bodies as temples of the Holy Spirit, and not merely to act, but to think, always as in His pure and searching presence. Will you say that under such a rule a man's range of thought would be restricted and his mind become narrow? Let the words of St. Paul to the Philippians be your answer: "Finally, brethren, whatsoever things are true, whatsoever things are honourable, whatsoever things are just, whatsoever things are pure, whatsoever things are lovely, whatsoever things are of good report; if there be any virtue, and if there be any praise, think on these things: . . . and the God of peace shall be with you."

In speaking of the relation of this principle to being, we are naturally brought to think of its important relation to *knowing*. It is only through this very same path of clearing away sin, or overcoming, and then seeking to be sound or pure inwardly, that we can find truth. The "bringing every thought into captivity to the obedience of Christ," which necessarily purifies, is the very condition precedent of knowing God. Indeed, it is by character, or, in other words, by seeking to be right before God, that we come to know God. Christianity, which is the truth about God, cannot be proved, and its truth known, by any other means. You are disposed, some of you, perhaps, to resent this statement. You demand that your reason should be convinced, that the objections and prejudices which block the way should be removed, before you can in any sense accept Christ. You are like one shut up in a dark room, who demands to have his reason convinced that there is such a thing as sunlight, and how it is and what it is, before he will throw open the windows and let it come in. He is withering in the darkness, when by simply pushing back the bolts and throwing open the shutters he might feel all the invigoration and know in himself all the glory of the noonday. There must be, as St. Paul affirms, the "casting down of reasonings and every high thing" in your mind, "which exalts itself against the knowledge of God." You can only begin to know, when you begin to obey. As the blessed sunlight is beating upon the closed shutters, so God is ready to shine into your heart. You cannot prove Him by argument. You can only know Him and walk in the light by yielding to Him—by letting Him come in. "If any man willeth to do God's will, he shall know of the doctrine, whether it be of God, or whether I speak of myself."

God's will is not to be looked for in some law outside of you. It speaks in your consciences. If you will but silence the tumult of your noisy prejudices, and bring your thoughts into an attitude of listening submission, you may know from moment to moment what God would have you do. All the faith required of you is to accept Jesus Christ for what He manifestly is, incarnate love, purity, and truth, and let Him be the Sovereign of your thoughts. However the world may rave about the Bible, whatever may be the defects of our theologies, doubt as we may much that is said and written and claimed for Christianity, that man cannot be wrong who takes Jesus Christ to be a law unto himself. If there be nothing else certainly true in all this wide universe, the spirit of that Man as it was in Him, and in all that it would make us, is truth to be trusted. Begin here, and in bringing every thought to the touchstone of His pure presence you will purify yourself, your nature will be spiritualised, your perceptions will be cleared, "the light of the knowledge of the glory of God in the face of Jesus Christ" will begin to dawn upon you. I will not attempt to describe the experience further; I feel too unworthy; I should seem to know more of it than I do. But I stand upon the shore; I see how it is possible for a man to realise the calm, deep heaven of the wondrous beatitude, "Blessed are the pure in heart: for they shall see God." It is like a mountain lake which I have gazed at with charmed eyes in the Tyrol. Majestic cliffs enclose it on every side and are reflected in its emerald depths. One seems to stand in mid-air, a world of majesty above, and another world of softened majesty and infinite depths of azure below. But when the surface of that lake is ruffled and its depths stirred by the tempest its peculiar charm vanishes; it no longer reflects the everlasting hills. When our hearts are swept by gusts of earthly passion, and turbid with pride and lust and selfishness, God cannot be known. When we cease our striving, and yield our thoughts to the " obedience of Christ," "the peace of God, which passeth all understanding, keeps the heart and mind." God is reflected in us; "the pure in heart . . . see God."

I have tried to show you how, by "bringing every thought into captivity to the obedience of Christ," we may overcome sin, be pure, and know God. I am afraid that we who preach, too often leave our hearers in doubt as to where and how they are to begin to believe in and obey Jesus Christ. They suppose that it consists in believing in a book, or obeying a set of precepts contained in a book; or they have a vague idea that it means not to do wrong, or to try very hard to be good. They think of something to be trusted or obeyed outside of themselves or up there. The simple truth is that the Christ we preach is to be looked for in our hearts. He is there, pressing upon us in impulses towards purity and right and love. The faith we preach is a simple giving up pride and opposition, and letting Him be the one ruling principle and passion of our inner life. The moment we let the sense of His love come in, we are compelled by the strong compulsion of a responsive love to "bring every thought into captivity" to His will. Yes; and the moment we begin in the silence of our souls to yield to Him, under the sunny consciousness of His great love, that moment God begins to live in us.

V.

The Love of God in Christ.

V.

THE LOVE OF GOD IN CHRIST.

The love of God, which is in Christ Jesus our Lord.
Rom. viii. 39.

I MET in my life as a pastor, many years ago, a man who objected to the language of the General Thanksgiving: "We bless Thee for our creation, preservation, and all the blessings of this life." He said that he was not thankful for his creation—that it would have been better for him if he had never been born; that his preservation had been only the prolonging of misery; while the blessings of this life consisted in pain, poverty, and loss. I told him that if the General Thanksgiving had ended there I should agree with him. But it does not. That which makes life tolerable, which enlarges our horizon, which clears up the mystery, is contained in the words following: "Above all, for Thine inestimable love in the redemption of the world by our

Lord Jesus Christ; for the means of grace, and for the hope of glory." Now it is of this inestimable blessing I would speak—"the love of God, which is in Christ Jesus our Lord." The apostle means not our love towards God, but God's love towards us, manifested for our salvation in Jesus Christ.

The question of God's disposition towards us can never cease to be one of importance to the average man and woman in this world. Notwithstanding the efforts of eccentric persons to get the idea out of the minds of men, the idea will remain, because we are subject. There is a power working in and through and over and outside of us. We are dependent upon it. We cannot escape from its control. We live and move and have our being in it. There are so many evidences of an intelligent will manifested in the working of this power, that we naturally give personality to it. The spirit in us which wills and thinks and reasons, reaches out instinctively towards some great Father of our spirits. It finds a voice in the words of the creed: "I believe in God the Father Almighty, Maker of heaven and earth."

Assuming, then, that there is an almighty Maker of heaven and earth, what do we know of His mind and purpose concerning us? Does He care anything at all about us, or are we, with our sensitive, conscious spirits, only atoms which He is whirling, crushing, grinding in the great mill of some vast purpose, regardless of our pain or pleasure? Are we to go whirling on through endless cycles, born into responsibility without our consent, and carried on whether we will or not? The beautiful creation outside of us does not satisfy. You cannot comfort suffering, struggling men and women by pointing them to a beautiful sunset. When I stand by the bedside of my dying child, agonised by his suffering, which I cannot relieve, and Heaven sends no help, will the flowers which some friend sends comfort me? They are but an aggravation of my misery. It is as if God smiled at me in my sorrow and mocked my helplessness. He does not touch me. The earth has indeed been made beautiful to my eyes, and is marvellously adapted to my physical needs, and even ministers to my pleasure; but I am worse off than the beasts, for they chew the cud of a present animal contentment, while I see in the fair creation something which mocks me—something which I cannot reach. We feel with Jean Paul Richter when he said of music: "Away! away! Thou speakest to me of things which in all my endless life I have not found, and shall not find." I have no evidence in nature that God cares any more for me and my kind than He does for the grasshopper or the worm. Fire, flood, tempest, lightning, earthquake, and avalanche are as reckless, apparently, of human life as they are of insects and beasts.

There is but one revelation of the mind of God which can reach the heart of man and glorify his life. It comes to us in the person of Jesus Christ. The truth which shines out from Him has its fullest expression in St. John's familiar words: "God so loved the world, that He gave His only begotten Son, to the end that whosoever believeth in Him should not perish, but have everlasting life."

Now I do not want to argue anything. My purpose is simply to set forth the mind of God as it is expressed in Jesus Christ, and to show

how different it is from any other manifestation of the invisible; how closely it touches us, and how powerfully it may affect us, if we will but yield to it.

And first, note that the love of God in Christ has personality. It enters into our humanity; it takes shape in history. "The Word was made flesh, and dwelt among us." "No man hath seen God at any time; the only begotten Son, which is in the bosom of the Father, He hath declared [or "interpreted"] Him." If God was ever to reveal Himself to man, who in all ages has groped after Him, what more likely than that He should come directly into our humanity? How should He be understood otherwise? Men in all ages have looked for Him in nature and clothed Him in terrible forms. Why should it be thought a thing incredible that He should manifest Himself in the highest part of His creation—human nature itself? Ah, say the sceptics, but it is incredible that the infinite power which pervades the universe should distinguish man, a mere worm of the dust, above all other creatures— that He should particularise him and stoop to enter into our flesh. Now just here is the fact in which man's shame and degradation consist. He has made darkness his element. He was worth caring for. There is a spirit in him which is related to the Infinite. But man had lost all sense of the divine possibilities which were his. This is the terrible fact of our condition. This is what constitutes our lost estate. Men scorn as a senseless theological dogma the teaching that they are conceived and born in sin, and yet find in a gross materialism, which credits nothing beyond the sensual and visible, their natural element. The fact that they will not see that there is a divine side to them, that they choose darkness and hug themselves in it and love it, is the fact that brought Christ into the world. The aspirations, the genius, the daring ambitions, the blind beatings against the cage which holds him, which appear through all man's unbelief, are evidences of the nobility of his origin. The old story of the prodigal brings out the truth of his condition in one strong touch: "He would fain have filled his belly with the husks that the swine did eat. . . . But when he came to himself, he said, How many hired servants of my father have bread enough and to spare!" He had been "beside himself" until that awakening moment. He had been satisfied with the husks and the swine.

Now Christ came to seek and to save that which was lost. He came to bring God back to man. His person, shining out a bright star amid the gloom of human history, means that man *is* distinguished above all other creatures. It is set in our midnight sky to guide our feet into the way of peace, because it tells us that when He touched our sicknesses with healing, and our sorrows with sympathy, and our sinful and remorseful conditions with pardon, and our fear of death with a promise that transfigures death, God was in Him. His life was God's way of speaking to us—speaking to us in human tones, in a human form that toiled and suffered with us, and saying to every needy condition of our life, "there is help, there is hope, there is love, there is life, there is immortality." We may always think of God, therefore, as being like Christ. We may understand what His love towards us means by studying Christ's words and works and character. We may know that it is a love which, while it makes no compromises with sin, yet yields its own Christ to the cross in order that the sinner may be pardoned. We may know that it is a patient, tender, pursuing, and unselfish love, entering into and touching every need and woe of our common life. We see it moving in One who was "a man of sorrows, and acquainted with grief," blessing the poor, feeding the hungry, healing the sick, weeping beside a grave, drying the tears of widows, gathering helpless childhood into its arms, carrying hope down among the very outcasts of society, and entering into a Gethsemane of agony in order that we might know, in the darkest struggles of life, that love is with us even there—there where it is so hard to say, "Father, not as I will, but as Thou wilt." Oh, is it not something that you may go to the New Testament, and know, as you study Christ in His relation to all sorts and conditions of men, that this is what God is towards you and all sorts of men now? It seems to me that one can bring his heart up to such a study, and rest it there, and find great comfort. It was not a weak, indulgent, effeminate love. How intolerant it was of hypocrisy—how it hated unreality, deceit, pretence! How it rebuked and put to shame by its own example selfishness! and yet how tender it was towards sinners, how slow to judge, how ready to forgive, how superior to the world's mean, carping, backbiting misjudgments!

I have said that because the love of God in Christ has personality we can understand it. But we could not take the love which Christ exhibited to be God's love if He had not proved Himself to be something more than human,—in other words, that which He claimed to be,—the Son of God. He was crucified, dead, buried. If the story had ended there we should have no evidence that God was in Him. He was, as Paul says, "declared to be the Son of God with power by the resurrection from the dead." This event carries Him out of time into eternity, out of the seen into the unseen, out of the past into the ever-present; and yet not out of history, for He is living in the hearts of all who have received Him, and in His Church, which is His body. He has passed in glorified human form into the presence of the Invisible, the representative of our race, and embodying in Himself that which He has made possible for every one of us.

We reach here a point of thrilling importance, which marks the love of God in Christ. It makes possible for us, through the same Christ, an entering into His own sublime relation of sonship with the everlasting God. This statement is no cunningly devised fable. May God help us to keep it disentangled in our minds from the dogmas of theology. It is one of the realities of the gospel, and the ray of sunshine which strikes most directly down into our common life.

He died, but His death was God's mysterious way of satisfying the avenging forces, and reconciling the guilty consciences of men to the thought of forgiveness in the Just and Holy One. He appeared on the other side of the grave in glorified human form—humanity clothed upon with the life of a higher sphere. In that form He appeared to Mary, and this was the message which He sent to His disciples—words which ring out as clear and sweet as village church bells on a summer day: "Go to my brethren, and say unto them, I ascend unto my Father, and your Father; and to my God, and your God." He had made it possible by His death for us to think of the Infinite as our Father as He was His Father, and as our God as He was His God. He makes it possible by His resurrection power—the power of His "life for evermore," the power of a divine Spirit—for us to become, as He was and is in very thought and feeling and character, sons of God. "As many as received Him," writes St. John, "to them gave He power to become sons of God, even to them that believe on His name." He is writing of that which took place after Christ had left the earth. Love's greatest work in Christ did not begin to be done until after He had vanished from the bodily view. It was the work of entering into men's souls and working life and resurrection there. This is what God's love in Christ would do for us now. It is moving for our help more powerfully and more universally even than when He walked on earth. " Touch me not," said He to Mary, " for I have not yet ascended unto the Father." It is clearly to be inferred that, having ascended, He can be touched as He could not be on earth. We may bring our spirits to Him, and realise healing and comfort and life, just as truly as they did who brought their blindness or their leprosies or their withered limbs when He walked through Judea and Galilee. But we must bring our spirits to Him. God's love will not do its gracious work for us if we choose to sit in the dungeon darkness of our selfishness and lust. There is Fatherhood in God brooding over all men, but the adoption of sons can only be for those who will open their hearts to God, manifested in Jesus Christ, and let Him take possession. It is a spiritual work now. We know Christ no more after the flesh. Our conception of God must always wear the character of that unique personality which has once for all in the historic record been projected out of eternity upon the screen of time. But to realise God spiritually now, we must let the full meaning of that personality take possession of our hearts. This is what St. John meant by receiving Him. This is faith in its simplest definition. Thomas, the doubter, illustrated it when, standing in the presence of the risen Jesus, the full meaning of His personality suddenly dawned upon him, and he exclaimed, "My Lord and my God." He had long been His disciple. He only received Him at that moment. "Blessed are they," said our Lord, "who have not seen, and yet have believed." To let the sense of God's love, disclosed in Jesus Christ, come into your hearts and rule there, that is faith. To live in the consciousness of a divine Fatherhood, and keep yourselves in it by acting as sons of God, are the simple conditions of realising the resurrection power of Christ.

But you turn away wearily, and say to yourselves: "This is not practical. How can we busy, toiling men and women, absorbed in everyday worries and a wearing struggle for existence, how can we be like Christ? How can we act as sons of God in a world like ours?" "His life was exceptional," you say. "He was a preacher and teacher, and went about doing good. We have domestic ties. We have to work for a living." Christ, I answer, was without sin; but He was human, and tried in all points like as we are. I sometimes think that He was so truly human that the full consciousness of His deity did not dawn upon Him until He rose from the dead. His life was not so unlike ours as we imagine. Remember that only three years of His life were lived in public ministry. He was first the ordinary infant of Jewish parents, born in a manger. He appears once, after twelve years, an eager, thoughtful boy, sitting in the midst of the doctors, both hearing them and asking them questions. A sense of some waiting, divine mission seems to have flashed out in the gentle answer to His mother's remonstrance: "Wist ye not that I must be about my Father's business?" But He went down, and was subject unto them. Eighteen years longer—thirty in all—He lived in obscurity, working probably at Joseph's trade; and yet all that time He was growing in that divine Sonship which bloomed finally upon the world's view—"the glory as of the only begotten of the Father, full of grace and truth." He did not grow away from God in the midst of the routine of daily toil and the struggle of a humble workman's life. When we see Him in His perfected manhood He is not dependent upon anything external to Himself for peace or comfort. He is calm amid the strifes of men, because the Father is with Him.

He is superior to fear and pain, and never murmurs at the hard conditions of His earthly life, because His real life is in the unseen and eternal. Worn to death upon a cruel cross, His last sigh is breathed in the words, "Father, into Thy hands I commend my spirit." Looking back now, we see that through the grave and gate of death He passed to a joyful resurrection. And now I say that He is the ideal man. I say that He has made it practicable for every one of us to live in just that same divine relationship of sonship with God as that in which He lived, and which made Him superior to time and sense and death. I say that we may carry into our workday life, as He did, the inspiration of our higher destiny, that we may live in His peace, and commend our souls at death to the same Father. It simply depends upon yourselves, your own wills, whether you will live in the sunshine of Christ's Father and your Father, of His God and your God; or whether you will shrink away into the earth, like creatures whose nature it is to burrow under stones and into dark, damp holes, because they love darkness rather than light. Oh, what would not the love of God, which is in Christ Jesus our Lord, do for us, if we would but let it come in! It would change the whole atmosphere of our inner, secret life. It would make us realise that our true life is in the spiritual and eternal. It would breathe into us a vivid consciousness that God is our Father really, and not merely in metaphor. The human fatherhood is the imperfect, reflected image of the reality in God. It would have us know that we may hide our failings and infirmities in the bosom of His great love, confident that if our purpose is honest He will understand and make allowances, even when short-sighted earthly friends censure and misjudge. It would make us both ashamed and afraid to sin, because sin is against love, and every cherished sin puts the obscuring of our own sense of guilt between us and life. It would fuse all duty and obedience into one glowing principle of love to God, working out in love to man. It would make us fearless of the threatenings of time, man, and death, in the certain confidence that we are " bound in the bundle of life with the Lord our God." It would clothe all nature with new and satisfying charms, because in all its forms, from the fragrant lily-of-the-valley to the lightning's red gleam, we should see love working—working life even through seeming death and destruction.

Time forbids me to go further. It would be easy to show how God's love in Christ, received into men's hearts, would solve every dark problem of their condition, lift them out of sin into new and divine relations, harmonise all the harsh discords of their social life by bringing it into unison with the spirit of Christ's command "that ye love one another, as I have loved you," disclose in sorrow and pain only such a discipline as He passed through who, "though He was a Son, yet learned He obedience by the things which He suffered," and rob death of all its terrors in the light of His rising, who shall change our vile bodies and make them like unto His own glorious body.

My friends, you know that the health of your bodies is affected by the atmosphere in which you breathe and live. You know, too, that in a moral sense your minds and manners are affected by the social atmosphere with which you may choose to surround yourselves. It is a matter of infinitely greater importance that you should consider what sort of atmosphere you habitually *think* in. I fear that many of us may find, if we go down into the secrecy of our souls, that we are breathing the stifled, poisoned air of selfishness, lust, or mere earthiness. There can be no life, light, nor salvation for us until we throw open the windows and let the great love of God, which is in Christ Jesus our Lord, come in and take possession of us.

VI.

Life in the Light of the Resurrection.

VI.

LIFE IN THE LIGHT OF THE RESURRECTION.

Wherefore we faint not; but though our outward man is decaying, yet our inward man is renewed day by day. For our light affliction, which is for the moment, worketh for us more and more exceedingly an eternal weight of glory; while we look not at the things which are seen, but at the things which are not seen: for the things which are seen are temporal; but the things which are not seen are eternal.— 2 COR. iv. 16–18.

LIFE looked very dark to St. Paul when he wrote these words. The world was against him. He was perplexed, persecuted, weary, and death stared him in the face. But he sees a bright side to all this. He counts the affliction light and for the moment, compared with the eternal weight of glory which it is working for him.

Where does he get this confidence? Where

is he standing, that he should be able to see glory gilding such conditions? He gets the confidence from a habit of mind which looks not at things seen, but rather through and beyond them to things unseen and eternal. He stands in the faith of a Christian, who endures as "seeing Him who is invisible."

Now I have no intention of arguing with anybody. This is neither the time nor the place for argument. The materialist and the infidel would "not be persuaded, though one rose from the dead." I only propose to set forth the habit of mind which Christianity would create in us, and to show that it puts us on the bright side of the darkest dispensations, and affords us a largeness of view and a largeness of living which make all other living seem small and pitiable.

There are things seen, and there are things not seen. This much, I think, every one must admit. That nothing exists but that which our eyes can behold is a manifest absurdity; for the very thought that thinks it, is invisible, and yet thought is. The life that is in every one of us cannot be seen, and yet life is.

The majority of people live under the dominion of things seen, and count it the only rational way of living. There is certainly much that is bright and beautiful for our eyes to enjoy. We have nature, with its myriad forms of softness and serenity, gentleness and power, beauty and sublimity. We have man's works, everywhere displaying skill, genius, enterprise—painting and sculpture, architecture, daring inventions, and innumerable lovely creations of his hand, rivalling nature itself. We have the world of humanity, with its lovely forms of childhood and youth and womanhood, to charm our eyes; with relations and associations of family and friendship which are precious to us; with its capacities for social excitement and pleasure, the song, the dance, the feast, the play of thought and wit, the converse of congenial spirits. Oh, yes, says youth; there is everything to live for in the things which we see. We are in this present visible scheme of things; why should we not enjoy it?

Shall I tell you that if you love the present world you will lose a heaven of bliss hereafter? A great mistake is often made, I think, by Christian ministers, and great harm done to their cause, by vague denunciation of something which they call the world and do not define. The impression is conveyed that Christianity compels a choice between the present world, in which we must eat, drink, toil, love, enjoy, and suffer, and a possible heaven of bliss in some far-off hereafter. I do not much wonder that some sceptics echo the sentiments of the old Persian poet towards Mohammedanism:

> "Some for the glories of this world, and some
> Sigh for the Prophet's paradise to come.
> Ah, take the cash and let the credit go,
> Nor heed the rumble of a distant drum."

Christianity does not set a possible future against a certain present. It is an entire misconception to suppose so. The heaven which it opens to the believer begins here and now. Its light comes in through the faith which opens to a perception of things unseen and eternal. Worldliness is living exclusively in and for things seen. Unworldliness is not ignoring the seen, separating yourself from it, hating it; but looking through it to the unseen, and living for that, and under the dominion of that, and with a view to that. Here is the real distinction.

"What shall it profit a man," said Jesus Christ, "if he shall gain the whole world, and lose "—heaven hereafter? no; but—" lose himself?" If you live only for the material,—the gratification of the senses, the enjoyment of that which you can see and taste and handle,—you necessarily starve all the higher faculties of your being. There is a side of your nature which would blossom towards the Infinite. It is capable of spiritually seeing God and living eternally in His light. But if you never open it towards things unseen and eternal, all these divine possibilities wither; unused, they die, like the eyes of fish in dark caverns, which through disuse have lost the capacity for seeing.

When you ask me, then, why you may not enjoy all that you see in this beautiful world, I answer that you may, and should, enjoy everything that is pure and lovely; but if you live only by the sight of the eyes, you miss the highest life—you lose your true spiritual self. And then what an uneasy, restless, unsatisfying dream life is, if there is nothing but the things seen! There is one fact about them which must be admitted, and which shuts us up under a sad, oppressive, ever-brooding mystery: "The things which are seen are temporal." The very earth beneath our feet, which we call firm, sometimes trembles, and makes shipwreck of our confidence. Youth soon finds that its bright hopes are graveyard lights, delusive will-o'-the-wisps, or the phosphorescence of decay shining in the night. Temporal! Yes; youth grows grave and care-worn and gray. The eyes of the wife or the child or the friend, that beam on us with love, fade. Their light goes out; we close them. They are gone, and we are alone! When we attain, we have lost the capacity for enjoyment. Change is everywhere. We may be thankful, when we think of the wrongs, crime, pain, and poverty which are in the world, that the things seen are temporal. We must die. If death ends all, the Epicurean maxim is wisdom: "Let us eat, drink, and be merry to-day; for to-morrow we die."

Let who will think this is rational and all that is possible for man. I say that the man who thinks and feels, who has a spark of anything which is not merely animal left in him, knows better.

But turn now to the more cheerful side of the subject.

There are things unseen and eternal. The trouble is that we are in such a material habit, so incrusted with material needs, thoughts, and desires, that we have come to believe that nothing can be real which cannot be seen. We do not dare to open ourselves to the invisible forces which are pressing upon us on all sides and sometimes break through in manifestations which startle us.

We feel them in nature. Back of the laws and forces which science discovers, every unbiassed thinker feels that there is Infinite Mind. What is it that makes almost a pain the ecstasy of enjoyment which we feel when we look into some lovely sunset sky, or breathe the crisp air of some mountain height, with the deep blue of space over us? What is it that makes us long to melt and lose ourselves in their brooding atmosphere of spiritual beauty and perpetual peace? Why do we turn back to the prosaic world sad, like some galley-slave who has caught the sound of far-off bells, and voices of the long-lost and almost forgotten home?

Is it not that, back of or within the visible, there is a spiritual something which is our birthright, and which we have somehow lost? The very rose that is sent to us in our sick-room has its greatest charm, it seems to me, in something that we do not see. We enjoy its perfume and lovely hues and delicate petals, but there is something more than its fading beauty. I always feel that it would tell me something—that it has a cheering message from somewhere. I think, if it could speak, it would tell me how lovely and full of love He is who thought a rose, and thought it for me! Is it my God?

Thoughtful men of all ages have been conscious of these unseen powers. They have built their altars to the unknown God. Not until God manifested Himself in Jesus Christ was heaven opened. This is the truth of Easter day—a truth in which all Christians must rejoice: "Life and immortality brought to light."

"Now is Christ risen from the dead, and become the first-fruits of them that slept." The historic Christ who was "born of the Virgin Mary, suffered under Pontius Pilate, was crucified, dead, and buried," burst the bands of death, left the tomb empty, folded up the grave-clothes, appeared to His disciples, then vanished out of their sight. The resurrection is just as much an authenticated fact of history as any other fact of His life. It is precisely that which might be expected from His character and works. He proved Himself, by this act, to be what He had claimed to be: "Immanuel—God with us." He is not merely a reminiscence, a historic character of the past, like Socrates or Plato, or Cæsar or Napoleon. He is a living Christ. He has passed out of time into the glory which He had with the Father before the world was. Divine, yet human—the God-man! The voice that comes back to us from Him to-day out of the unseen declares: "I am He that liveth, and was dead; and, behold, I am alive for evermore, and have the keys of Hades and of death." "This is our God. We have waited for Him, and He is become our salvation." He is alive for us—alive that, through His brotherhood with us, He might make us know and feel that we are sons of the one Father. "Go," said He to Mary, "and tell my brethren that I ascend unto my Father, and your Father; and to my

God, and your God." Alive, that we may know that there is a world beyond time and sense. "In my Father's house," said He to His disciples, "are many mansions; I go to prepare a place for you."

Here, then, is the light that is ready to shine into our hearts out of the unseen and eternal—"the light of the knowledge of the glory of God in the face of Jesus Christ." To look not merely at the doctrine about Christ, nor at the Bible which reveals Him, but to look in the face—that is, into His divine personality as the New Testament reveals Him—is the first step towards the light. To throw down our prejudices, and let that personality, in all its perfect beauty, take possession of us, to trust it as a living personality, living for us and in us, to stand, in a word, where Thomas did, and say with a sense of personal appropriation, "My Lord and my God"—that is faith.

Standing here, we begin to see and feel the power of things unseen and eternal. Nature and the present world remain, but they are transfigured. The sun is on them now. "The things which are seen are temporal." Yes;

death is here. Nature has lovely phases, but it will blast with its lightnings and overwhelm with its avalanches, earthquakes, and torrents thousands of human beings, reckless of youth, beauty, innocence, or virtue, sweeping them away as if they were ants! In vain do we think of the God behind nature and life as a tender Father when He seems so reckless of human life and suffering.

But when we see all this in the light of the resurrection, we can understand that death is not the worst thing that can happen to us. Christ entered into the agony of the garden and the cross; He was permitted to die a cruel death, though He was "the only begotten of the Father, full of grace and truth." But death was only an incident of the divine life which was to triumph over it. He entered into our human conditions of suffering and death in order that we might, through Him, triumph over them. We make too much of death. It is but an incident of the life in us that lives on when the body falls away. It is the dissolution of the material which sets the spirit free. It is the breaking of the cage that lets the imprisoned bird fly. It is the dropping of the withered autumn leaf, that the new budding life beneath may spring. What shall I fear, then? Let come what may of desolation, pain, death, "our light affliction, which is for the moment, worketh for us more and more exceedingly an eternal weight of glory." "I am the resurrection, and the life," saith the Lord: "he that believeth on me, though he were dead, yet shall he live: and whosoever liveth and believeth on me shall never die."

Realise the meaning of these sublime words, and think what a terror vanishes, what perplexities which seem to contradict God's love are removed, and what infinite possibilities are opened to us. But beyond all this, think of the new meaning which the dearest relations of life take on, when we look through them to the unseen Christ and the eternal possibilities in Him. The hardest experiences in life, perhaps, are those in which we have to see vanish into an awful silence loved ones who are parts of our very being. Father, mother, brother, sister, child, are ties which bind us to all that is purest and happiest on earth; but looked at in their visible forms they are temporal. They must die, and we must die. When the sorrow comes we are apt to think, if we do not say, "What does God know about it? He is a far-off abstraction. He cannot understand a poor, bereaved mother's or father's love!"

Ah, just here we make a mistake. What right have we to separate ourselves from the great Father in whose image we were made? Christ entered into our human conditions for the express purpose of making us know and feel that the Father does know and understand our sorrows. "If," said He, "ye, being evil, know how to give good gifts unto your children, how much more shall your Father which is in heaven give good things to them that ask Him?" See! He authorises us to do something which we are always afraid to do—reason up from our pure human affections to God. If you can love so, how much more the infinite Father who is the spring of this love! If He has created a mother's love to be the soft, protecting cradle of infancy, surely we may be confident that the everlasting arms are underneath when our children pass away, and that they are folded into infinite tenderness. We are comforted by the tears and kind ministries of our friends. We are always thinking that our friends are kinder than God. We never think that He can be like that. But are not they parts of God, as the rose is an expression of God? To bring us back to a consciousness of this fact, from which sin had divorced us, He expressed Himself to the world in the human form of Christ. He was our brother in the flesh, entering into all the conditions of our life, from childhood to the bitter cry in the garden, "Father, if it be possible, let this cup pass." He is the same now in His risen glory. Uniting in Himself the human and divine, He is ever for us the expression of God, and we know from His ministry on earth how He could pity and weep and love and suffer. He is nearer to us all than when He was on earth, by His Spirit pervading the hearts and lives of His people. He is present with us in all those precious, unselfish, loving ministries which touch us in our sorrows and needs. We are too prone to forget that the spirit of love which is present in the world, providing homes for the orphan, the widow, the sick, the needy, going about doing good, working quietly through thousands of faithful women, making itself felt in little rather than great acts, and in unconscious influence as much as by direct effort — we forget, I say, that Christ is in all this. It gets its impulse from the beating of His great heart against the hearts of those that trust Him.

Well, then, if there really is a Father who lives so near us in the known person of the risen Jesus, why should we not be confident that the forms which are so dear to us are only fading into the realities of a larger life for them and for us? Why should we not be patient

> "Till
> The night is gone;
> And with the morn those angel faces smile,
> Which we have loved long since, and lost awhile."

Do you not also see, that which I have not time to dwell upon, that the mixed circumstances and events of the world and of our individual lives, which seem utterly confused and dark and hopeless when we, like one lost in a fog, are entangled in and under them, appear simply as the writhing of the morning mist in the valley before the coming glory of the day, when we look at them in the light of His eternal purposes, to whom one day is as a thousand years, and a thousand years as one day? I have often stood on mountain-tops, and, seeing the mist rolling below, have thought how gloomy it must be to dwellers in the valley. They were under the clouds. They could not realise how transient they were, but I knew how the sun was working through them; I knew that they were but for a moment.

I have read somewhere of an Athenian so wise that the most difficult questions which could be devised failed to perplex him. A certain young philosopher boasted that he could outwit him. He proposed to hold a little bird concealed in his hand, and then to ask him if it was alive or dead. If he should answer, "Alive," he would crush it and say, "No; it is dead." If he should say, "It is dead," he would open his hand and let it fly. He held the bird in his hand, and put the question, "Sage, is it alive or dead?" The sage answered, "It is as you will!"

My friends, you have it in your power to let your spirits fly or to crush them in an earthly grasp. Whether they shall live eternally in the sunshine of God's smile, or die, does not depend upon argument; it is not a question for the intellect to determine. If you are in sympathy with that which is pure and noble and unselfish and true, you will open your hearts to Jesus Christ and say, " My Lord and my God." The question of life or death for your soul is a moral, not an intellectual, one. " It is as you will! "

VII.

Staying by the Stuff.

VII.

STAYING BY THE STUFF.

As his part is that goeth down to the battle, so shall his part be that tarrieth by the stuff: they shall part alike.—1 SAM. xxx. 24.

ZIKLAG was the dwelling-place of David and his followers during their temporary sojourn in the country of the Philistines. It was at that desperate period in his life when the madness of Saul made him an outlaw and forced him into entangling alliances with Israel's foes. He had left the town with his little army and joined the forces of the Philistine king, Achish. But the presence of the Hebrews created distrust in the Philistine camp, and they were obliged to march back to Ziklag. They reached the city only to find it a smoking ruin. The Amalekites, a neighbouring people, had seized the opportunity which the absence of the warriors afforded to revenge previous depredations upon their own borders. Wives and children had been carried into captivity. Desolation reigned where they had looked for rest and love and plenty. Their grief knew no control. They wept until they had no more power to weep, and then turned in wrath upon their leader, and muttered fierce threats against him. It was a moment of bitter agony for poor David. His soul might well cry out, " All Thy waves and Thy billows are gone over me." Outcast, bereaved, plundered, and now menaced by his own followers, it was no weak faith which enabled him to look away from flesh and earth and " encourage himself in the Lord." Divinely taught, he found in immediate action an outlet for the angry feeling which threatened to burst upon his own head. The storm was turned against the spoilers, and, forgetting hunger and fatigue, moved by the thought of their dear ones' wrongs and the hope of rescue, the little band of six hundred started in quick pursuit. Now two hundred of their number fainted by the way. Their hearts and wills were strong to go on, but their weary feet refused to carry them. The brave remnant, disencumbering themselves of every unnecessary article, left "the stuff" in charge of their exhausted comrades at the brook Besor, while they pressed forward. They surprised the Philistines as they were feasting in their camp, scattered them with great slaughter, rescued unharmed their wives and children, recovered their lost possessions, and gained a great spoil besides. Triumphant and rejoicing, they turned back to their waiting comrades at the brook. Here, in mutual congratulations and the reunion of parted families and friends, joy reached its height. But the happiness of that hour was marred (as the same cause has marred domestic joy in many an age since then) by a question of property. Certain grasping sons of Belial claimed that those who had not gone down to the battle should have no share in the spoils. It had been pain to the fainting ones to linger. It was their misfortune, and not their fault. They were not to be held accountable for that which God had allowed for His own glory and they had not willed. They had honestly "done what they could." David, recognising the cruelty and injustice of the claim, interposed his authority. His decision became a statute and ordinance in Israel from that hour. "Ye shall not do so, my brethren. . . . But as his part is that goeth down to the battle, so shall his part be that tarrieth by the stuff: they shall part alike."

It was the principle which David's greater Son unfolded when He said: "He that is faithful in that which is least is faithful also in much." It suggests some truths which are commonly overlooked, and which are full of meaning for that large class of persons whose lives move in a routine of quiet, ordinary, every-day duty. We need do little more than state the general principle that service is a universal duty. David and his men had a work binding upon every one of them to do, and all were called to it; but a difference in ability made a diversity of work. So all men are called to serve God. Whether we will serve Him, or not serve at all, is really not an open question. We must, by the very necessity of our constitution, serve some master. Idleness in the sense of pure quiescence is, for a rational creature, impossible. The indolent man is one of Satan's busiest instruments. The machine works steadily on through its appointed time. If we do not occupy the soul with useful thoughts and purposes, it wears upon itself and works out its own destruction. The man who lives to pamper his own desires is a creature of the flesh. He who chooses wilfully to commit sin is the slave of sin. The world and the flesh and sin are chief captains of the prince of darkness. Idleness, therefore, is merely a voluntary assignment of ourselves to evil. Self-indulgence is a farming for the same master—" sowing to the flesh, and of the flesh reaping corruption." Wilful sinning is direct service with hire; its wages " is death." Man is not left free to choose between the yoke of Christ or no yoke at all. The question is, Whom shall he serve? Shall I be the slave of the evil one, or the free and loving child of God? The service of children—children of God by faith in Jesus Christ—is that to which we are called. For this service we were made. By it the highest end of our being is reached, and its fullest development attained. To bring us back to the knowledge of it, and make us again capable of it, Christ lived and died. It is true that " by faith we are saved," but faith creates the noblest kind of action, because it inspires love. Love cannot be otherwise than fruitful in good works. Faith without works is certainly dead, and the Christian who has felt the glow of a living faith must keep it alive by yielding to its unselfish impulses, or the life will certainly die out of him. Exercise is quite as essential to the health of the soul as it is to the health of the body. The spiritual feebleness, melancholy, and indifference of not a few who call themselves Christians is wholly due to stagnation. We have marked with delight the effect of zeal for some good work stirred up in such sluggish souls. Shaken out of their selfishness, they forget their morbid grievances, and become bright with hope and glowing with life. The movement is like the flow of a river. When the tide is at its height, and just idling before it turns, there is scum upon its surface. The debris which the inflowing waters have brought up clings to its banks and makes deformity. But the current turns, and then all this unhealthiness is borne out and away. The river sparkles and is pure and glad again. Let a fervent love tide through your heart and go out in corresponding deeds, and the mass of doubts and fears and morbid feelings which obstruct and breed disease will be swept away, and the spiritual life roll on, ever increasing in peace and purity, until it meets the sea.

But we come closer to the immediate principle of our text, and remind you again that varieties of capacity and condition occasion manifoldness of service. Some are compelled to stay " by the stuff " while others go down to the battle. Those fainting ones whose grief it was to linger and be passive by the brook, represent a large class of earnest Christian souls. They are troubled because they cannot do some great thing. They associate acceptable work with high philanthropic effort or the self-denying missionary life. Thus, straining after lofty deeds, they are in danger of overlooking the duty which lies at their door. The Church of Christ may be compared to the complicated wheel-work of a watch. There are tiny levers whose action is scarcely perceptible; there are passive screws and rivets whose virtue it is to be fixed and firm; there are wheels which move fast, and wheels which move with a measured, monotonous, retarded movement; but each smallest piece is necessary to the proper adjustment and operation of the whole. The beauty and utility of the thing depend upon the exactness with which every part, however trifling apparently, fulfils its appointed office. There are some among Christ's people who have wealth and all the attendant opportunities for exerting influence and dispensing charity, while others are surrendered to poverty and its hard conditions. Some are blessed with health and vigour, while the life of others is an hourly struggle with pain and feebleness. Some have, by educational advantages or natural gifts, large intellectual abilities, while others move in a more restricted sphere of thought and have but one talent. If we judged as men judge, by the bare outside, we might conclude that only a favoured few have opportunities for service; but when we look over the field as it is in God's sight, and consider that He gathers into His remembrance the ordinary and the extraordinary, the unnoticed and the conspicuous, the active and the passive alike, ah, then we know that there are possibilities of service in every sphere.

The opportunities for extraordinary deeds are few. They are not often found by those who seek them. Men rise to them out of and over ordinary things. If we wait for them we may waste a lifetime and go empty-handed into the presence of our Judge at last. But ordinary duties press upon us always and everywhere. Not an hour passes in which we may not harvest something for our Lord. The little child may glean side by side with the strong man in this field: opportunities to make some one happy eagerly improved; faithfulness in business or home duties; words of counsel or of comfort spoken in season; considerateness for others as it may be shown in a thousand ways; little attentions and kindnesses; the sweet allowances of charity; and the word of peace which quiets strife. There is no honest place or station in which we may not glorify Christ in a service of love; and a life in which every day is luminous will be more beautiful than the meteor-flash of some showy deed which goes out in blackness.

We have thrown into contrast also the *unnoticed* and the *conspicuous*. The world has been blessed, especially in these latter days, with munificent givers, whose lavish benevolence has blessed whole cities and won the admiration of two continents. Shining philanthropists, too, have adorned history in the persons of brave men and gentle women, who, while not courting applause, have gone down into plague-houses and prisons, and upon bloody battle-fields, to carry light, love, and healing. The names of devoted missionaries, daring persecution, hardship, and death for Christ's sake, are also fresh in our memories. But for every one of these whom God has fitted to " go down to the battle " there have been a thousand, with hearts as warm and consecrated and loving, whom circumstances have compelled to tarry in the household and the shop: mothers grown gray in toiling, watching, enduring, worn with the daily dripping of home cares, untiring in ministries of love; mechanics bound to the anvil or the bench, their life a plodding, wearisome routine, and yet strong in character, influential for God and the right, and serving as truly by skill and faithfulness in the daily work as the preacher by his preaching; children left to struggle with the desolation and poverty of orphanhood, but strong in the promise, "When my father and my mother forsake me, then the Lord will take me up"; merchants thrown among the dangerous eddies of the money circle, involved in manifold anxieties, but "fervent in spirit, serving the Lord," manfully standing for the truth against sceptical opinions, and steering an honest course through subtle temptations; helpers in irreligious households, faithful and consistent through manifold humiliations, patient under the bitterest of all persecutions, sharper than the knife,—the tyranny of the tongue,—that which an apostle calls "trials of cruel mockings." These are not forgotten before God. The family, the school, the counting-house, the shop, the farm, are fields which may yield as rich a harvest of good works and precious influences as heathen lands to the missionary. They demand a work as costly, and heroism as great, as that which goes into the prison and onto the battle-field. They are less conspicuous; but the numberless rills which flow in unseen shady places are quite as essential as rivers which float navies on their bosoms.

We enter the most obscure and yet the most affecting sphere of service when we consider the *passive* contrasted with the *active*. It is easier to do than to suffer. We are thankful for the little bands among us who are fellow-workers unto the kingdom of God. Their activity is a pastor's comfort, and health to their own souls. But activity is not the only measure of service. It would be better for some, perhaps, if they withdrew more often into the sanctuary of the still hour, and bathed their strong energies in prayer and meditation. There are passive graces blooming in the solitude of many a sick-room, hidden from the world's notice like flowers which spread their beauty and fragrance for God only, in regions where no human eye ever intrudes,—which are seen and noted by the Father. God is sublime in His patience. Christ was never more divine than when, under the most cruel provocation and before the most insulting accusations ever heaped on man, "He answered never a word." The most heroic service of His life was in that moment when He cried, "Father, not as I will, but as Thou wilt."

To be enfeebled or deformed, and see others

straight and vigorous and useful; to feel one's self an object of pity, or a burden and unsightly in the eyes of our fellows, and be patient; to be laid a helpless invalid upon a bed whose rest becomes torture, and hear the roar of the busy world outside, the merry laugh of children, the tread of many feet along the pavement; to see the free sunlight and catch glimpses of the blue sky, and know that we are barred out from them hopelessly, and yet be cheerful, trustful, even happy,—oh, who will say that this is not service—service acceptable to God, wonderful in the sight of angels?

I think of one, a worn and wasted figure, who for more than twenty years was stretched upon a couch of pain. Says Dr. Arnold, speaking of his sister (for it is to her we refer): "I never saw a more perfect instance of the spirit of power and of love and of a sound mind, intense love almost to the annihilation of selfishness, suffering a daily martyrdom, yet of herself wholly thoughtless (save only as regarded her ripening in all goodness); enjoying everything lovely, graceful, beautiful, high-minded, whether in God's works or man's, with the keenest relish; inheriting the earth to the very fulness of the promise, though never leaving her bed nor changing her posture; and preserved through the very valley of the shadow of death from all fear or impatience and from every cloud of impaired reason which might mar the beauty of Christ's glorious work. May God grant," he adds, "that I may come but within one hundred degrees of her place in glory." I think of another, well known to me. For more than half a lifetime she was a helpless cripple; the movement of a finger was pain, and she had to be carried about her house and to her carriage like a child, in the arms of an attendant; but never once did a murmur escape her lips. She was cheerful almost to mirthfulness. Her soul was luminous with the life and peace of the gospel, and her tongue and pen eloquent, and never weary, in telling the good news to others. None came within her influence, even for an hour, who did not take knowledge of her, that she had "been with Jesus." Though so helpless, the poor were reached by her, an institution reared for the most depraved among them by her zeal, and many a strong man was put to shame by the fervency with which that one bent, disfigured, tortured yet happy woman served the Master. Similar instances, doubtless, suggest themselves to my hearers. The cheerful submission of such sufferers is a silent gospel. Who can fairly estimate their patience, faith, and love, and fail to perceive that

"They also serve who only stand and wait"?

Now, to this wide field of service, comprehending those who "tarry by the stuff" as well as those who "go down to the battle," the principle of David's ordinance applies: "They shall part alike."

We estimate deeds by their magnitude and quantity. God estimates them not by quantity, but by quality. He is not won by noise or show. He looks at the spirit of our deeds. Their merit is determined by the faith of which they are the expression and the love which moves them. They called it a waste when Mary, out of the fulness of her loving heart, poured the precious ointment upon Jesus' head; but He said: "She hath done what she could"; and, "Verily I say unto you, Wheresoever this gospel shall be preached throughout the world, this also shall be spoken of for a memorial of her."

The outer court of the temple, in which stood a brazen chest inviting the offerings of the people, was once thronged with those who had come up to the feast. In a retired place, where He could rest Himself and watch the passing throng, sat a quiet observer. The rich and the great swept over the marble pavements and cast in largely of their abundance. As their gifts fell, they rang out the givers' praise, and a look of proud satisfaction gleamed over their faces, and the bystanders said, "What liberality!" But there came a meanly attired woman. She crept shrinking up to the box,—she would have hid herself if she could,—and dropped in noiselessly two mites—the merest trifle, but it was all that day's living. She passed out unnoticed, or noticed only to be despised, save by that one quiet observer. He called His companions to Him, and pointing to her said: "Verily I say unto you, This poor widow hath cast in more than they all."

That observer was God in Christ, measuring

a deed by its interior principle. He teaches us how vast a trifling act may be. The world has crowns for those who make a noise and a show; but before God "there are first who shall be last, and there are last who shall be first." It is the world of thought and motive which lies open to His eye, and His benediction rests upon faithfulness in every condition. We may make the commonest tasks illustrious by doing them in His fear and to His glory. It is one of the divinest features of the gospel that it strikes through those flimsy effects which dazzle and deceive men, and, waking up the buried manhood which is in us, bids us be great by what we are, and not by what we wear and have and seem. It sets before us the praise of God as the grand goal to be attained, and that is won by no rank, purchased by no wealth, but open to every condition, the reward of the faithful.

If, then, we are hemmed in by circumstances which leave us only quiet, ordinary work to do, let us carry the spirit of the Master into it and by intense faithfulness make it Christian work. If our station does not adorn us, we may adorn our station. It is by going on in just that line of things wherein we stand that the Lord would have every department of life reached and leavened, and so, too, we prove ourselves worthy of grander things and pass into wider spheres; as David, faithful as the shepherd boy, and Joseph, true to God as Pharaoh's slave, mounted at last to thrones.

And this is the sort of demonstration which the world needs now. The battle for the historic truth of the gospel has been fought. The times demand a vivid exhibition of the power of the living Christ in the hearts and lives of men. Preachers and scholars alone cannot give to the age the argument which shall be most potent to establish the kingdom of our Lord. It must come from the store and the counting-house, the workshop, the factory, and the family. It must be the product of faithfulness in those that stay "by the stuff" as well as in those that "go down to the battle."

"They shall part alike." Yes; when the battle is over, the victory won, and all the ransomed marshalled upon the plains of heaven, the earnest Paul will scarce outshine in glory the loving Mary; I do not think that the holy Samuel will wear a richer diadem than the faithful Hannah; the saints of Cæsar's household will receive as hearty a "Well done!" as the noble army of martyrs. The one test will be, "Have you improved the talents, be they little or much, which I committed to you? Have you done what you could?" Only be sure and live for God. Any other life is unworthy of you. He calls you first of all to believe on His Son Jesus Christ; believing, you have life; and living, you love; and loving, you do Him grateful service. Do not be satisfied with the world's praise. There are short roads to popularity and fame. You may live to win them and have your reward. But your life will have been a mere stage effect: a brief hour before a fickle audience, the transient applause, and the curtain falls; the scenes are folded up. You have performed your part and had your reward. But you have done nothing real. The light of eternity reveals the bare beams, the tawdry decorations, the pulleys, and the paint. You stand before your God as you are, not as you seemed to be. He reckons with your thoughts, your motives—in a word, your character. Disguises are stripped off. Your real self is laid bare. You gained a corruptible crown which turned to dust upon your brow, but you have lost the incorruptible crown of God's favour, which is life everlasting.

Whatever, then, your condition, be it wealth or poverty, weakness or strength, youth or old age, enlightenment or ignorance, begin just where you are (so that it be an honest place) to live for God. Have no fears for the issue. "The race is not to the swift, nor the battle to the strong"; "but as his part is that goeth down to the battle, so shall his part be that tarrieth by the stuff: they shall part alike."

VIII.

Does God Care?

VIII.

DOES GOD CARE?

And they awake Him, and say unto Him, Master, carest Thou not that we perish?—St. Mark iv. 38.

THE Lord Jesus Christ had been preaching to the multitude on the western shore of the Lake of Galilee. This lake, or sea, as it was called, though only thirteen miles long, and six miles wide in its broadest part, was a busy place in His time. Its waters abounded in fish of all kinds. Two of the many villages which thronged its borders derived their names from the fisheries. Bethsaida (signifying "the house of fisheries") was the home of Philip and Andrew and Simon. All of these villages sent forth their hardy fishermen by hundreds over the lake. When, in addition to these, we imagine the busy ship-builders, and the many boats of traffic, pleasure, and passage which were moving upon it, and then the beach at the base of green mountain slopes, sparkling with the houses and palaces, the synagogues and temples, of the Jewish or Roman inhabitants, it is easy to realise that the whole scene was full of life, enterprise, and energy. It was along this sandy beach, which completely encircles the Lake of Galilee, that the people thronged to hear Christ, and often followed Him when He sought to retire in a fisherman's boat to the other side. The other or eastern side of the lake was an unfrequented region, broken by deep ravines, and inviting to rest upon its green, grassy uplands. He had, it would seem from St. Mark's story, been speaking to the crowd from one of the boats moored just off the beach. All day He had taught them "many things by parables." The same day, when even was come, He said to His fisher friends: "Let us pass over unto the other side." They took Him, "even as He was in the ship," and made sail for the wilder region on the eastern coast. Worn out, He sank down upon the helmsman's cushions at the stern of the boat, and fell asleep. The sky darkened, and through one of those deep ravines which break through the hills to the shore a thunder-gust swept upon the frail craft. Every one who is familiar with such waters knows how suddenly these squalls come, and how quickly a threatening sea rolls up. The Lord Jesus Christ slept calmly on through the plunging of the boat and the wild, drenching sweep of the waves which began to fill it. "Master," cried the disciples, "carest Thou not that we perish?" We might suppose that this cry was only an instinctive effort to arouse One whom they loved to a sense of their common danger, were it not for the appeal which seems, according to the other evangelists, to have been mingled with it: "Lord, save us." They evidently expected help from Him, and wondered that He could sleep through such a storm. He awoke, and rebuked the wind, and said unto the sea, "Peace, be still"; and the wind ceased, and there was a great calm. Then He turned to the disciples, and the remarkable fact is, that instead of commending them for "calling upon Him in the time of trouble," He reproved them, saying, "Why are ye so fearful? how is it that ye have no faith?" He turned from the stilling of wind and wave to the tempest of fear in their souls, and rebuked it as something more perilous and more difficult to subdue than the raging of the sea.

The prayer to Him in their moment of peril, "Lord, save us," was certainly an expression of faith. Why, then, did He reprove them for lack of faith? The point is that He would have had them trust Him without a miracle to attest His power. They were fearful when it should have been enough that He was with them in the ship. It was a very weak faith, from His standpoint, that could be terrified by mere physical dangers. He would have had them serenely confident through storm or calm, sinking or surviving, living or dying. It was too much to expect of poor human nature then. The disciples learned the lesson later when a new Spirit had entered into them. The purpose of His reproof was to teach them and us that God cares, even though He may not work miracles to save us from the present storm.

Does God care? That is the question which the incident brings vividly before us. There is no greater need, I venture to say, for every one of us, in this changeable, storm-swept world, than to know that God cares. It may be a matter of indifference, even, whether there be a God or not, to the young and strong and prosperous, whose skies are cloudless, and under whose keel the waters babble gaily, while hope with soft, fragrant breezes fills the sails. But the world is not like that all the day. Changes come before the eventide. For the multitude, the story of the voyage is a tale of angry clouds and toiling in rowing, and the psalmist's cry, "All Thy waves and Thy billows have gone over me." To the struggling, sorrow-tossed multitude the question of an invisible Father caring and working for our good through all the seeming evil is vital and related to our deepest needs. We need no stronger evidence than the records of despair and then suicide which daily meet our view. It is not difficult to perceive in the progress of the world or society in general that there is, as in nature, an ordering purpose, evolving some ultimate good out of the seeming chaos. But it is not of the general development that you and I care to hear. Does God, if there be a God, care for me? That is the question which voices itself in the deep silence of my soul, and it is fraught with tremendous importance in its bearing on my character and happiness and destiny.

We were made for sympathy, just as we were made dependent upon this atmosphere in which we breathe and live. The limits of our physical being are very narrow indeed. A few miles above the earth, as you know, we should cease to be; and there is only a grave for us beneath its surface. As our bodies exist only in this special atmosphere, with its certain range of temperature and balance of elements, so our intellectual, moral, and spiritual being exists and is tolerable only in the social or sympathetic condition. Men may scorn the expression of a craving for sympathy as weak, and be too proud to admit their need of it; but the fact remains that we live and move and have our being in it. No punishment can be inflicted upon a man more terrible than solitary confinement. Shut out from the society of his fellows, his starved mind gnaws upon itself, and he becomes a maniac or an imbecile. Suddenly eliminate from human life all that comes to us from association with our kind in business and in pleasure, in our home relations, in the warm glow of friendship, in the touch of mind with mind, and what have you left? Frozen clods, just as if the radiant energy of the sun's heat died out of our atmosphere.

But human sympathy does not reach and satisfy the deepest needs of our being. There are experiences, known to every thoughtful man and woman, in which we must either get breath from God or stifle in our loneliness; experiences into which our best friends cannot enter, which may not be described, which could not be understood. Every one of us, far back in the secrecy of his own self-consciousness, is alone with griefs that cannot be told; with disappointed loves or ambitions; with a bitter sense of misjudgment or an agony of regrets for a past which cannot be recalled; with secret sins that tear at the conscience, though we smile among our fellows; with the throbbing pain of bereavements which no balsam of earth can heal; with the gathering gloom and isolation of the thought that old age is fast settling into the chill night of death around us; with doubts and fears towards God and eternity, and hate and distrust, perhaps, towards our fellow-men. Worse than solitary confinement in the dungeon of a prison is the state of that man who, without hope towards God, is shut up to the brooding, spectre-haunted loneliness of his own soul. Jesus Christ sounded the lowest deep of human woe when for a moment, hanging upon the cross, He lost that which had sustained Him through all His lonely ministry on earth, and cried out in His agony, "My God, my God, why hast Thou forsaken me?" What is there for us in the loneliness of guilt, if we have no faith to pray, "God be merciful to me a sinner"?—in the loneliness of sorrow, if we have no confiding sense of One who can be touched, and who is working as a Father for our good?—in the loneliness of pain, if we cannot get breath to cry, "God help me"?—in the loneliness of the world's misjudgments, if we cannot turn to One who knows the heart and judges righteously?—in the loneliness of age, and then of death, if we have not the faith which looks onward with hope to the new day, and sings, "I shall be satisfied when I awake with Thy likeness"?

I have tried to illustrate the very great importance of the question, Does God care? I must pass to the point which is the essence of the whole matter, and which is so strikingly shown in the story of the stilling of the tempest. *It is no evidence that God does not care because He sleeps while we seem to be perishing.* This was the truth which the disciples had not faith enough to perceive, and which He reproved them for not perceiving. We think, as the disciples did, that it would be a supreme evidence of the being of a God, and the reality of His care, if He would always show Himself awake by some direct answer to our cry for deliverance from pain, loss, danger, or death. Assuming that the purpose of the Creator, in our being, were to care for our bodies and their development in all material good, we might expect material deliverances. We might naturally say in our hearts, "There is no God," if no answer came to our call for help. But the purpose of the Creator in us is not our mere physical wellbeing. We are body, mind, and spirit. The body is only the base of a temple whose special beauty is in the parts which rise above the earth. It is evident to the feeblest intelligence that a wise and good Creator could not grant every wish of a creature limited in knowledge and capacity. The relation is the familiar one of parent and child. The child must often cry for that which the parent, in his wisdom and love, cannot grant.

But there is more to be said than this. If the gift of God is eternal life, and if we are capable of almost infinite development towards that life in mind and spirit, then the supreme evidence of God's care must be, not the mere stilling of tempests and healing of diseases, but the presence of His power in our souls to calm the raging of our passions and our fears, and to breathe upon us the peace which passeth all understanding. Now, to bring us this supreme evidence of God's care, Christ came into the world,—" God manifest in the flesh,"—lived, taught, suffered, died, and rose again. "In this," says St. John, "was manifested the love of God towards us, because that God sent His only begotten Son into the world, that we might live through Him." He did not come into the world to be merely the physician of our bodies, and to multiply our loaves and fishes, and to save us from physical death. The "Peace, be still" to that tempest on the Lake of Galilee was only an outward and visible sign of the inward and spiritual purpose which He would work out in our souls. It is a striking fact that our Lord never wrought a miracle to help Himself or to satisfy His own physical needs. The tempter found Him hungry after the long fasting, and said: "If Thou be the Son of God, command that these stones be made bread." He answered: "It is written, Man shall not live by bread alone, but by every word that proceedeth out of the mouth of God." He would not allow the transient suffering of hunger to force from Him an exercise of divine power which would have been, on His human side, as the tempter knew, distrust of God's care. He might, as He said, have called down twelve legions of angels to help Him in the garden of His agony; but the faith of a perfect manhood showed itself in this patient cry: "Father, if it be possible, let this cup pass: nevertheless, not as I will, but as Thou wilt." How entirely human He was in His shrinking from the cruel pain which was before Him! But the cup did not pass. He had to drain it to the very dregs. He did not, however, question the wisdom or the love which was silent when He seemed to be perishing. The disciples thought all would be lost if their ship went down. His ship went down in the storm of Gethsemane, but all was not lost. He triumphed through that which we call perishing. It was no evidence to Him, you see, that God did not care because He slept while Christ seemed to be perishing. He did not judge of His Father's love by the material help which He gave, but by that conscious, abiding, spiritual power which enabled Him to say, "Thy will be done."

Now it is precisely so that we, in the light of the resurrection, and of God's purpose to lift us out of an earthly habit into an undying life of the Spirit, are to judge of God's care. It is no evidence that He does not care because He permits us to suffer. There is love in the suffering. Trials must be. They begin with the tottering steps of the child, who through many a fall learns to walk, and through many a painful experience with cuts and burns and bruises learns to live. They are necessary incidents of an imperfect human condition. Time and space and the restrictions of the flesh harness upon us the hard necessities of toil, struggle, study, pain, weariness, sickness, and then death. Many of them we bring upon us by our own fault. But through these incidents of our environment we learn to subdue the lower and reach to the higher. Mind overcomes matter, manhood in its distinctive nobleness is developed, and so it is all along the line up to the spiritual. We "learn obedience," as Christ did, "by the things which we suffer." Experience which comes through suffering teaches us that to obey God, as He reveals Himself in nature, in our consciences, and in Christ, is the way to life. Faith is a necessity (not intellectual belief, but personal trust in the invisible Father), because we cannot see the end nor pierce to the eternal blue through the earth-born clouds which overshadow us. The worst trial of all—death—which seems to us to be perishing, is, in the light of God's truth, not perishing, but a passing into life. He has mercifully sent Christ to teach us this. There may be infinite love, therefore, in the bereavements which break up our earthly ties, and the final event in which we seem to be perishing may be only a happy flight from the cage. I think nearly all of those fishermen disciples who were so terrified by the storm on the Lake of Galilee passed through the cruel suffering of a martyr's death. No help came to them, but they did not cry, "Lord, save, or we perish." They knew better then. They knew that God's care is not to stay the course of suffering or death, but through it to make us know that there is a life beyond, and through faith, hope, patience, experience, purity, truth, and love to educate us for it.

The man who quarrels with his environment and will not heed its lessons, nor reach on to the life towards which they point, is lost. He yields himself to the present and the sensual. He comes under the fierce power of his passions. All the splendid possibilities of his intellectual and spiritual being, like some richly freighted vessel driving uncontrolled upon a rocky shore, are in danger of perishing. Yes! there are storms and a shipwreck possible within you, infinitely more to be dreaded and more difficult to subdue than any blast which might wreck the body. If the trial of your life is a body wronged by excesses, by dissipation, by drink, by sensuality, broken down, feeble, racked with pain, do not doubt God's love because, when you cry, "God, help me!" in your misery, He does not by a miracle restore your diseased body. He would be a party to your sin if He did. You must look for His care in the peace and pardon which He would speak to your soul. The suffering of the body is the sharp discipline which would drive you back to Him, and happy is the man who bears it patiently and learns the lesson. It is in this case, as in every other, no evidence that God does not care because He sleeps while we seem to be perishing; rather is it an evidence of His love.

I ask you, in conclusion, to look at Christ *asleep on the pillow* while the storm darkened and the waves came surging into the plunging vessel. The timid sleep lightly and wake at the least alarm. The guilty dream and start. Christ was neither timid nor guilty. His Father was with Him waking, and like a child He slept, with no shadow of fear on His soul. He was human in His weariness, and He is our human example in the perfect calm of His repose. When they awoke Him, He arose, not with terror in His look, but only surprise that they should be fearful. An ordinary man would have sprung to his feet startled, and rebuked his crew for not waking him before. This extraordinary man arose in the majestic consciousness of superiority to the raging elements, and, commanding them to be still, they obeyed Him.

I think that this whole scene of the reposing and the storm-stilling Christ is a parable of the repose and the control which He has made possible for us in our relation to the stormy elements of the present evil world. The difference between our Lord and His disciples in that hour of trial on Galilee was this: the disciples were in mind and spirit under the dominion of the wild elements, and cried, "Save, or we perish"; the Christ was in mind and spirit superior to these elements, and knew that if they did their worst they could not wreck the life which was in Him. To them death seemed the end of all. To Him death was only the breaking from a chrysalis state into the winged life of an endless summer day. This is the salvation which Christ brings, and the supreme evidence of God's love, that it is made possible for every one of us through faith in the Lord Jesus Christ, to live in calm superiority to every threatening element of time. The man who has no trust in any word or will of God from beyond time is like the disciples under the earth-born clouds. He sees in death, and in all the various incidents, accidents, and ailments which lead to it, only perishing. He loses all when the body fails. There is no hope nor comfort in the suffering which surges round him when the property, friends, amusements, or other objects which minister to the body fail. Save him from loss, grief, pain, death, or he perishes. These to him are absolute evils. There is no merciful purpose in them; neither is there anything beyond them.

The man who believes is, like Christ, superior to the storm. "This is the victory," says St. John, "that overcometh the world, even our faith." Why faith, faith, always faith, do you say? The simple answer is, that it is faith which trusts where we cannot see, and realises the power and presence of the Invisible. We may not expect God to still the winds and the waves which threaten us as we cross the turbulent ocean; but we may be fearless and calm in the confidence that the very worst that they can do cannot destroy us. These and other physical dangers we may not be able to subdue; but we may, in the faith of Christ, forbid that they should subdue us. To kill the body is nothing, if there is an indestructible life of the spirit within it. We come under the power of physical ills only when we allow our spirits to be made afraid by them, and our hold of God and of His truth to be shaken loose, and the darkness of despair to settle down upon us. We may not expect that God will uniformly work miracles of healing for us in answer to our prayers, though the prayer of faith may save the sick; but far more important, a greater blessing which He will surely grant to those who seek, and which He seeks to give, is the saving of our souls from that clinging to the flesh which makes sickness and old age and death-beds terrible. The real victory over pain, sickness, and old age is to be seen in that man or woman of whom, in the words of an apostle, it may be said, "though the outward man is decaying, the inward man is renewed day by day."

But why do I talk any more of the body and its pains and trials and inevitable decay? Christ's miracles were simply the bringing back of the perfect and natural order into the unnatural disorder of a sin-cursed world. They said: "What manner of man is this, that even the wind and the sea obey Him?" He has put it in our power to do a greater work than this. What matter a few years of suffering in the flesh, and then death, if our souls are saved from the eternal death which comes by sin? The storm we have to fear is that which springs from our selfish and sensual passions. The victory which He would give is the power to keep under our bodies and bring them into subjection. The manhood which is possible for us is a manhood like His, which, though it may feel the strain of temptation, is so strong in the consciousness of a higher life and its thoughts, hopes, loves, studies, pursuits, that it bids the winds of passion and the raging of bodily appetites and fears be still, and they obey.

If your manhood is only secular, present, animal, —only in the body and its conditions,—then all goes down when the body sinks. Whatever survives the wreck must be a pitiful lost thing, a vagrant in the spiritual world of purity, love, and God.

Does God care? Yes; He cares so much that He will not make the present transient period of existence easy for us. He cares so much that He forces us to realise that this is not our rest. How blind we are not to see that this is the meaning of our trials! He cares so much that He would not still our mere outward tempests, but would enable every one of us to be the stiller of the tempest of sin in our souls; so that, in the strength of His presence and power, we may defy death, and through all life's discipline develop the character which belongs to heaven and shall survive the wreck of worlds. There will be no need of mere physical miracles when the earth has dissolved and the perfect order reigns, for we read in the Revelation that there shall be " no more sea, . . . neither sorrow, nor crying." " They shall hunger no more, neither thirst any more; the sun shall not light on them, nor any heat." "The inhabitant shall no more say, I am sick." "All tears shall be wiped away; and there shall be no more death." One miracle shall remain, the miracle of the redeemed soul, the miracle of the man or woman who has overcome sin, the flesh, and the world. These shall form the white-robed company before whom the angels stand wondering, "who came out of great tribulation, and washed their robes, and made them white in the blood of the Lamb."

IX.

The Temple of God in Us.

IX.

THE TEMPLE OF GOD IN US.

Know ye not that ye are the temple of God, and that the Spirit of God dwelleth in you? If any man defile the temple of God, him shall God destroy; for the temple of God is holy, which temple ye are.
—1 Cor. iii. 16, 17.

THESE strong words were addressed to the church at Corinth. This church was simply the body or congregation of believers in that busy commercial city.

Human nature is the same in all ages, and the church at Corinth eighteen hundred years ago was remarkably like the church at Washington or any other locality to-day. It was far from being a temple of God in fact. The very purpose of St. Paul's epistle was to quiet party strifes, reprove gross immoralities, correct errors of faith and practice, and bring back members of the church from a secularism, sensuality, and formalism which were polluting the sanctuary of God. He does not attempt to judge between the parties which divided the church. High, low, broad, ritualistic, and rationalistic were all there, under other names. He is not jealous for his own name, nor envious of the eloquent Apollos, whom some had set up as his rival. "Is Christ divided?" he exclaims, "was Paul crucified for you?" He drives through their contentions and the envyings and luxury and drunkenness which defiled even the sacrament of the Lord's death, and indignantly arraigns them for their blind carnality in having lost the sense of God's high purpose in them as a church. "What, know ye not that ye are the temple of God, and that the Spirit of God dwelleth in you?"

These words were addressed to the Christians *collectively*. He calls upon them to remember that they are a temple builded together to realise a divine idea among men, a unity in righteousness, a sanctuary in which a holy God might manifest His love. He appeals to them as a general might appeal to the *patriotism* of his soldiers in some crisis of a nation's history.

We forget, as they did, that we are *members of a body*. By every obligation of our baptismal, confirmation, and sacramental vows we are not to consider our individual selves alone, but ourselves in relation to the whole Church. No man liveth unto himself, and it is impossible that any member of the Church should live unto himself. The Church, which is Christ's body, is honoured or dishonoured in us. If a man is a mere narrow, pharisaic formalist, an ecclesiastical partisan without the Spirit of Christ (which is the spirit of love) in him, he is a disintegrating influence; he tends to mar the unity of the temple. If he is an indifferent, worldly member, satisfied to attend church and partake occasionally of the sacrament, but with no thought or interest for the kingdom of God among men, he dishonours the Church; he is a selfish, disloyal citizen, without the patriotic fervour which is a nation's strength. The question, therefore, my friends, of the rightness of our individual lives as members of the Church is not to be determined by the evil which we actually do, but by the good which we leave undone. Of course we are not to do wrong, but the Christian idea is something far higher than this. It is positive loyalty to Christ and His kingdom in lives which shall not merely be blameless, but heroic for goodness, truth, and right.

I need not, however, dwell upon the application of these words to Christians collectively. It is the aggregate of personal lives that makes the one strong nation and the one strong Church. To realise the positive idea of a kingdom or temple of God among men, each individual Christian must think of *himself* as a temple made for God's indwelling. St. Paul passes, in this same epistle, to this close personal application of the thought of our text: "What, know ye not that your body is the temple of the Holy Ghost, which is in you?"

The structure of the whole Church, and of each particular church, is like the cell structure in plant life. The plant is a complex organism made up of many cells. The life of the plant is in these, and depends for its growth upon the functions which they perform in accumulating and distributing nutriment, and imparting health and beauty to the whole.

So the Church is one temple, "the blessed company," as our Communion Office defines it, "of all faithful people"; but it is made up of countless little temples or sanctuaries — the personal lives of its members. The character of the whole is determined by the spiritual richness and fulness of these separate lives.

God comes into the Church, then, through us — through the sanctuary of our spirits. He no longer dwells in a temple made with hands. St. Paul uses the word in the Greek which signifies, not the whole Temple building in Jerusalem, but the most holy place or sanctuary. The most holy place or sanctuary now wherein God waits to reveal Himself is the spirit of man. "The kingdom of God," said Christ, "cometh not with observation: . . . lo, it is within you."

What, then, are we doing with ourselves personally? Are we keeping ourselves open towards God, or are the windows of the dome of our being all crusted with dust and cobwebs through long disuse, so that the light of the blue heavens overarching it cannot shine through? Where do we, in the deep silences of our personal consciousness, habitually live?

Do we have our being in this beautiful upper room, and order all our living by its heavenly light? Do we keep the windows of the soul clear of the least thought of sin which might defile them, and do we estimate the world beneath us by the infinities above?

I am afraid that not a few of us who profess to be Christians treat the sanctuary of their being as some people treat their best room. They live in the kitchen, and the parlour is the coldest and most desolate room in the house. It is opened only occasionally, when there is a funeral, or formal company. There is a large, handsome Bible on the table, which is kept reverently dusted, but seldom opened. I associate, to this hour, with a certain stately room known to me in childhood, the coffin and the corpse.

Is it so that we treat the best room in this tabernacle of our flesh? Is it a place where darkness and death abide, while we really live in the lower rooms of our being, where everything savours of meat and drink, and the petty interests of the flesh, and the gratification of self? With what indignant reproach do the words of St. Paul come resounding down through the ages to us—"Know ye not that ye are a sanctuary of God, and that the Spirit of God dwelleth in you?"

Do you call yourselves Christians, and do you not know that if you have ever sincerely begun to believe, the Spirit of God is in you? Do you not know that the secret of power for you, and through you for the whole Church, is not in what you do outwardly, but in what you are inwardly? Ignorance of the sublime possibilities of our awakened nature, the capacity for receiving God, and being inspired with holy thoughts by Him, is to St. Paul a *shocking ignorance*. We may expect the sceptic to discredit as foolishness the suggestion of such spiritual capacities; but what shall be thought of the church-member who, magnifying the importance of receiving the bread and wine of the Lord's Supper, is blind to the hidden meaning and purpose of the sacrament expressed so fully in the sacramental office itself: "That we, and all others who shall be partakers of this Holy Communion, may worthily receive the most precious Body and Blood of Thy Son Jesus

Christ, be filled with Thy grace and heavenly benediction, and made one body with Him, that He may dwell in us, and we in Him." How often does the sublime sense of these words pass over our minds like living waters over the insensate rock!

The defect in our Christianity is that we look for God too much outside of ourselves, instead of realising that He is Spirit and that He makes Himself known in the far-back sanctuary of *our* spirits. Prayer, acquaintance with the word of Christ in the reading of the Bible, attendance upon church services, and partaking of the sacrament, are all means to the one end, and that is the indwelling of God. But merely to say prayers, to read as a formal duty the Bible, to attend church, to partake with the lips of the bread and wine, will not realise for us this indwelling. These are necessary means of grace, but it is the preparation of the heart in us which alone can make them effective. Prayer is more than asking; it is communion with the divine Spirit in our spirit. Paul does more than charge us to read the Bible; he says: "Let the word of Christ *dwell in you richly* in all wisdom"—assimilate it, digest it, meditate upon it to do it, and then it will be ever flowering in suggestions from within you for every time of sorrow and of need. And so, too, in our church-going and in our holy communion, the mind must be ready and receptive, or no divine influence will bless us.

In the use of all these means, the mind or heart is like the sensitive plate of the photographer behind the lens in the dark camera. The plate must be prepared and ready. No plain glass or soiled film will receive the impression. It is a remarkable and recent discovery that the sensitive plate, carefully prepared, will reveal to the astronomer through the telescope, stars which the human eye alone, though aided by the greatest magnifying power, could not detect. Invisible stars have thus impressed themselves upon the photographic plate, and have been brought to view in the enlarged print. Our souls, sensitised by a real, honest sorrow for sin, and faith in the love which pardons,—opened towards God by being cleared of every guilty purpose and wilful entertaining of sinful thoughts, and kept habitually sincere before Him,—are prepared to receive impressions from the invisible. "Eye hath not seen, nor ear heard, neither have entered into the heart of man, the things which God hath prepared for them that love Him. But God hath revealed them unto us" (if our hearts have been prepared and ready) "by His Spirit."

I have been addressing members of the Church. It may be supposed by those of my hearers who make no profession of religion that the words of the apostle have no application to them.

It is true that St. Paul writes to avowed members of the Church. There is, however, truth in his words which applies with equal force to you who make no profession.

Each one of you is a sanctuary for the habitation of God. The Spirit of God is striving to break through the earth-born clouds which veil it. Sometimes you catch a gleam of the clear heavens and the Light which, St. John declares, "lighteth every man that cometh into the world."

Emerson, in his famous essay on the "Over-soul," is very suggestive, the more so because he was a free-thinker, standing outside of the Christianity of the churches. That man is to be pitied as something which has sunk beneath itself who has nothing in him which responds to these crisp sentences. He is like Nebuchadnezzar, the proud king,—born to majesty, made to stand erect in the full glory of crowned manhood,—grazing in the fields with dumb cattle. "Our faith," says Emerson, "comes in moments; our vice is habitual. Yet there is a depth in those brief moments which constrains us to ascribe more reality to them than to all other experiences. We grant that human life is mean, but how did we find out that it was mean? What is the ground of this uneasiness of ours, of this old discontent?"

Yes; it is true, you who do not call yourselves Christians often feel that your lives are mean. In your moments of remorse, self-loathing, sorrow, or sickness,—in your lonely moments when you would not for worlds let your boon companions know what you are thinking,—you despise yourself. What despises? You—the something within—your other self, which looks at yourself with contempt. A quaint old poet well expresses this duality of our nature, though he sacrifices grammar to rhyme:

> "Within my earthly temple dwells a crowd:
> There's one of us that's humble, one that's proud;
> There's one that's broken-hearted for his sins,
> And one who unrepentant sits and grins;
>
> "There's one who loves his neighbour as himself,
> And one whose every thought is fame and pelf.
> From much corroding care would I be free
> If once I could determine which is me."

This higher consciousness is the divine Spirit in us, making itself known in the darkened sanctuary of our being.

What are you doing to yourself in all your persistent disregard of this divine Spirit, and persistent stifling of its suggestions? There is terrible meaning for all of us in Paul's warning words: "If any man destroyeth the sanctuary of God, him shall God destroy." By a necessary and natural process, the man who habitually sins against his body, or against his conscience or the impulses of his spiritual being, is destroying himself. It is not necessary to point to a judgment to come. The judgment begins here and now. The victim of avarice, hungry for gain, the miserable drunkard, the low sensualist, may enjoy a wild frenzy of passion; but who that knows anything of life, does not know that the debased body is burned out even to the mercy-seat in the Most Holy Place. The "Light which lighteth every man that cometh into the world" vanishes amid unholy flames, and at last the man sits in darkness and ashes, " having no hope, and without God in the world."

Despise not then, my friends, the words which would make real to you your capacity for an endless life in the spirit, having its centre in God.

Working through all the evil which is seething in the great caldron of the world to-day, there is the cleansing influence of such a movement towards the knowledge of God as the world has never seen before. Thirty years ago, in my own early ministry, scientific thought was thoroughly materialistic. To-day the men of science have become conscious of the fact, and admit, that they too must explore the darkness if they would seek the answer to all their larger questions; they too must assume the intangible if they would take any firm steps in explaining the series of facts with which they have to deal. When representative men in science and philosophy stand reverently before Christ,—when one of them, writing of "the destiny of man," and voicing the thoughts of many others not avowed Christians, admits that "the dream of poets, the lesson of priest and prophet, the inspiration of the great musician, is confirmed in the light of modern knowledge,"—when he tells us that, "as we gird ourselves up for the work of life, we may look forward to the time when in the truest sense the kingdoms of this world shall become the kingdoms of Christ, and He shall reign for ever and ever, King of kings and Lord of lords,"—I thank God and take courage. The reverent scientist, philosopher, or theosophist may not move in my lines, but they are moving towards the knowledge of God; they are moving towards the one centre of unity,—"seeking after God, if haply they might find Him." Some of them stand, like Philip before the Lord Jesus Christ, and begin to perceive the truth of His divine personality in His answer to Philip's demand, "Show us the Father": "Have I been so long time with you, and yet hast thou not known me, Philip?"

We reach to-day the last Lord's day of the year. Another wave of time is sinking into the past, and a few more hours will find us riding upon the swelling crest of a new year. Time— what is it? It is the brief moment in which we touch soundings as we pass from eternity to eternity. I fear that many of you think of time and the world as your all. All your thoughts and hopes and desires and interests are bound up with them. The fatal spell of the present has been cast upon you, and nothing is real to you but your eating and your drinking, your ambitions, your money-making, and your pleasures. When old age creeps on, and the chill shadows fall, you are wretched; death is a terror; the end seems to you only a fearful leap into the dark. I take up the words of St. Paul, and ring them as a New Year's peal in your ears: "What, know ye not that ye are the temple of God, and that the Spirit of God dwelleth in you?" Will you let the Spirit die out within the earthly tabernacle as you make the brief passage from eternity to eternity? The old Norseman kings, when they were about to die, had their bodies placed in a slowly burning ship, with all sails set, that, so passing out to sea, their death might be a vanishing into the elements, and not a rotting into earth. How much more should we, in the light of Christianity, be true to ourselves, and so estimate the present that, when we put out to sea, death shall be to us that which it waits to be for every faithful soul—" mortality swallowed up of life."

X.

The Temple and the Street.

X.

THE TEMPLE AND THE STREET.

In that day shall there be upon the bells of the horses, HOLY UNTO THE LORD.—ZECH. xiv. 20.

CONSPICUOUS in the beautiful dress of the high priest of Israel was a crown of pure gold, upon which was inscribed, "Holy unto the Lord." The skirts of the splendid robe of blue which he wore were hung with golden bells. When he passed within the awful mystery of the holy place the sound of the bells was music from another sphere than that of the common life of the people outside. Religion was localised. The sacred and the secular were far apart in the mind and life of the Jew.

The man who wrote the prophecy of our text, five hundred years before Christ, was certainly gifted with perceptions wonderfully far-reaching. He was a chief mover in the restoration of the Temple after the return from the Babylonish captivity. There was not much enthusiasm. The people were disheartened. They had grown faithless towards their Temple and their God. Zechariah, though he worked to restore the Temple, perceived that a time was coming when the music of God's own sphere should not sound remotely from the tinkling bells of the high priest within the veil, but out in the busy street, amid the stir and traffic of society, there should be upon the bells of the horses, "Holy unto the Lord."

The prophecy began to be realised when, at Christ's death, the veil of the Temple was "rent in twain." The awful sanctuary in which thunderings and lightnings and earthquake had seemed to be smouldering was opened to the day, and out of them emerged a life—a perfect life—the life of the man Christ Jesus. The old Temple, with its distinctions between clean and unclean, its cumbrous ceremonial, priestly caste, and separateness from the common daily life, vanished. "Destroy this temple," said the Christ, "and in three days I will raise it up." "But He spake," we are told, "of the temple of His body." That was raised up, and, as we know Him now in the light of the resurrection, we see the unveiled glory of God in the face of One who was in all points tempted like as we are—" the man Christ Jesus."

God in the ordinary human life is the new temple. This is the meaning of the Incarnation. The world has been very slow to perceive it. The prologue to St. John's Gospel declares it in the familiar words: " He came unto His own, and His own received Him not. But as many as received Him, to them gave He power to become the sons of God, even to them that believe on His name." Power or the right to become sons of God is the new impulse which the gospel has brought into the world.

Have you ever thought, in your average struggling workday lives, what this means? Have you ever thought that it is your revealed right, and made quite possible for you, to live up to the sense of an infinite Fatherhood as Christ lived up to and in it? This is Christianity; this is the salvation which, through the gospel, is preached unto you; this is the faith which can alone overcome the present evil world and the flesh and sin.

The truth I want to urge upon you is that the temple in this sense of God manifested and sovereign in every believing soul is necessarily related to the street. It has been over and over again argued that Christianity is incompatible with the ordinary business of life, that society could not exist if its principles generally prevailed, and that the wheels of human progress would be clogged. Honest thinkers are beginning now to perceive the deeper meaning of Christ's teaching, and to admit that the objection has sprung from prejudiced, ignorant, and superficial views of that teaching. It has been commonly supposed that the supreme purpose of Christianity is to save our souls from the impending torment of eternal fires after death, and that we can only be saved by a certain kind of faith which involves self-denial, the renunciation of this present world, a literal following of Christ in His poverty and suffering and ministry, and living solemnly in the presence of that awful doom of eternal burning into which thousands of our fellow-beings are dropping off every moment. I do not wonder that, in view of such a distortion of the gospel of

Jesus Christ, sceptics have argued that it is not compatible with the present business of life. But it is a distortion; and though it contains elements of truth, it is as far from truth as the grotesque image of a beautiful face which a concave mirror gives, is far from the truth of that face.

The supreme purpose of the Christ was not to save our souls from some eternity of torment hereafter, but from sin now. The eternal consequences of sin wilfully persisted in must be bad enough, but it is a present disorder; and to restore the lost order by bringing us to a sense of the infinite Father's light and love was His purpose. Self-denial is a necessary part of it, because we can live up to the higher only by denying or overriding the lower. The world to be renounced is the world of wrong, impure, and selfish principles, which have made the visible world of mankind itself a hell, and which He would make right and bring into harmony with the music of God's sphere, even the eternal law of love. The Christ we are to follow is the spiritual Christ, walking in love, "as He also loved us, and gave Himself for us." It was to save us from the flame of our own consuming lusts that He died. It was to win for us the heaven of a present peace, hope, and life that shall know no death, that He took our nature upon Him. The man who believes in order that he may save his soul from everlasting torment and gain a heaven of bliss hereafter has no true conception of the faith of Christ. "Honesty is the best policy"; but Archbishop Whately well said that "the man is a rogue who acts upon it." He would steal if he dared.

Christianity is more than a policy; it is a life. "I am come," said the Christ, "that ye might have life, and that ye might have it more abundantly." For one word in which He points to the eternal judgment for sin I can point you to a hundred in which He preaches the coming of a kingdom of God among men. We are not taught to be always thinking of saving our souls from death, but to "seek first the kingdom of God, and His righteousness." We are not taught to pray, "O Lord, save our souls from eternal fires," but this is the prayer which the Christ has given us: "Our Father which art in heaven, Hallowed be Thy name. Thy kingdom come. Thy will be done, as in heaven, so on earth." It is a creed as well as a prayer for the every-day life. He came "preaching the kingdom of God," and sent forth His chosen disciples to preach the "gospel of the kingdom." His aim was to create *in the world* a society of spiritual men and women, open to God, inspired by high, unselfish motives, realising their infinite relations, and touching humanity, as He touched it in the every-day life, with healing, helping, sympathetic, and uplifting influences.

The faith of the gospel, therefore, does not require you or me to be anything else but faithful and full of loyalty to God in just those relations and just that life (so that they be honest) in which we stand. We are not called to live Christ's life literally, as some satirists, to the detriment of Christianity, would have us suppose. We are called, however, to live His life spiritually in the sense which the Apostle Paul, writing to the Ephesians, has with a luminous pen defined. "Be ye followers of God," he writes, "as dear children"; and then immediately he shows them how they are to be followers of God—by being pure as men in their relations to a corrupt age, faithful as wives, husbands, children, slaves, and masters. You will find the same great apostle in all his epistles resolving the most seemingly abstract philosophy of the Christian faith into the practical duties of every-day life, and not seeking to revolutionise society, but summing up all in this charge: "Brethren, let every man, wherein he is called, therein abide with God."

Such is the spirit of the gospel of Christ. If it is not compatible with the average life of humanity, it is because the average life is shut up under conditions which the gospel seeks to break through, as the sun through clouds, to bring in a new day of light, life, hope, and love.

Christianity has already, in spite of the misconceptions and ignorance even of its friends, taken hold of the world powerfully. The humanities of our modern life—caring even to prevent cruelty to dumb beasts, honoring womanhood, abolishing slavery, tending to put an end to war, making human life sacred, blossoming into countless institutions of charity, responding with a world-wide sympathy to every appeal of human suffering, agitated by every problem that concerns the rights and well-being of men—are directly in line with the evolution that Zechariah dimly foresaw when he wrote that there should be upon the bells of the horses, "Holy unto the Lord."

I think it must be admitted, however, by every thoughtful man who looks out over the world of mankind, that it is capable of being improved. If some men love darkness rather than light, it does not follow that light is not good nor capable of dispersing darkness. "This is the condemnation," wrote St. John, or probably the Christ Himself, "that light is come into the world, and men loved darkness rather than light, because their deeds were evil." We see in the world to-day minds evidently in darkness, groping, stumbling, unhappy, and often desperate. We see sensuality holding its wild orgies in the light of lurid camp-fires, which passion has kindled, and which the pure dawn of God's day would put to shame. We see selfishness lurking everywhere—in capital, in labor too, in every form of business, in politics, in the church, and in domestic life. There is much light, hope, purity, and unselfishness, but I am arguing that society is capable of being improved. What will help, if not *the faith* that the destiny of man is to be something more than an animal, something more even than the genius of the brightest intellect that illumines the world—something, in fact, which the Christ, by His incarnation, death, and resurrection, has made possible for us, "heirs of God, and joint heirs with Christ"? What can help, if not *the hope* that in and through this present scheme of things there is a kingdom coming which shall be for all who enter into it an eternal uplifting, carrying them over death into the immortality of that "new heavens and new earth in which dwelleth righteousness"? What can help, if not that which is born of faith and hope—*love*, the universal love, the pure love of generous, kindly, honest sympathy and helpfulness? There was wondrous wisdom in Paul's words, "But now abideth faith, hope, and love, these three; and the greatest of these is love."

Yes; these three are capable of making sweet the bitter waters of our social life. There is many a good man who says within himself, "I must try to get all the help I can from my church and the Sunday rest to keep me through the week." That is not the best idea of the Christian life. He is like the diver, who takes in a supply of air to go down under water, and soon comes up exhausted. The Christian who has fully entered into the life of faith walks upon the sea of every-day life. Faith, hope, and love are vital elements in him. He has his being in them. He is buoyed up by them in his business every day of the week. He rests upon the pleasant isle of Sunday, but does not go plunging down on Monday into the depths of secularism, to breathe artificially and come up again at the end of the week nearly if not altogether smothered, and with really no superior spiritual life in him at all.

My brethren, it is for you and me to seek with all our might the realisation of Zechariah's prophecy, and bring about the time when there shall be upon the bells of the horses, " Holy unto the Lord." What nobler work — what aim more worthy of your manhood — can I set before you? God, I have said, in *the ordinary human life* is the new temple. To let God be in you by receiving Jesus Christ as the manifested God, and by living up to the ideal which He has set before you of a real sonship with the eternal Father, yielding yourself to the splendid consciousness that you are not mere animals or earthworms, made to grub and die, but children of God and of the resurrection, destined for an immortal society of which the present is only the germ—*this is your faith.* It is not necessary that you should be preachers or hermits in order to bring the street into harmony with the temple. It is only necessary that you should be true men and women, living in the sense of something above the mere toiling and moiling and bargaining and fretting and money-making which absorb you every day. The something above will regulate and calm and make holy all the common things.

> "There are, in this loud, stunning tide
>   Of human care and crime,
>   With whom the melodies abide
>   Of the everlasting chime;
>   Who carry music in their heart
>   Through dusky lane and wrangling mart,
>   Plying their daily task with busier feet
>   Because their secret souls a holy strain repeat."

Ye men and women who call yourselves Christians, and ye other men and women who do not call yourselves so, are temples in and by whom holiness may be carried into the street. If there is no sound of life in your temple,—no bells echoing from the great High Priest who has passed into eternity,—God help you! There is no sadder vision in all the universe than a man without God—defiled, hopeless, doomed. If you have life in you, the life of faith, hope, and love, *live* it every day and in every relation. It will lift you above care. It will make the world the happier for your being. You will be one wave—a very little one, perhaps, but still an impulse—in that sea of life which is setting in towards the blessed time when "there shall be upon the bells of the horses, HOLY UNTO THE LORD."

XI.

The Worth of Manhood.

XI.

THE WORTH OF MANHOOD.

What man shall there be of you, that shall have one sheep, and if this fall into a pit on the Sabbath day, will he not lay hold on it, and lift it out? How much then is a man of more value than a sheep!
ST. MATT. xii. 11, 12.

THE Christ was in a synagogue of His people on the Sabbath day. The Pharisees were seeking to involve Him in some violation of their Sabbath law, which would be a capital offence. A man was there who had a withered hand. They knew how quickly His heart could be touched by the sight of sickness or infirmity. It was a strange and suggestive fact that disease could not continue in His presence. They asked Him if it was lawful to heal on the Sabbath day. He turned to them, doubtless with indignation burning in His look, and said, "What man shall there be of you, that shall have one sheep, and if this fall into a pit on the Sabbath day, will he not lay hold on it, and lift it out?" It was lawful to save a sheep on the Sabbath day. They knew very well that for their own selfish interests they would do it. "How much then is a man of more value than a sheep!" The shaft struck home. It was like the thrust which He gave them when they brought to Him a woman taken in adultery: "He that is without sin among you, let him first cast a stone at her."

His argument was unanswerable. The whole Sabbath question was lifted into the positive atmosphere of love. "If you would rescue a sheep because it is your personal property, how much more is it lawful for me to lift a man out of infirmity on the Sabbath, and restore him to self-help and usefulness among his fellows!" There is a deeper thought than that which appears upon the surface: "You would rescue a sheep because it is your property. I am come to seek and to save that which was lost. Manhood is my property, and therefore I have a right to save men whenever and wherever and however I will."

The *worth of manhood* is the deep underlying thought of this whole scene which I want to urge upon your attention.

It is a strange fact that through all the course of this world's history a sheep has been reckoned of more value than a man. The sheep stands for property, or that which we may get for our own profit. The thought of *getting* rather than of *being* has certainly been dominant in human life, both individual and social.

Look at the individual life of our kind, and what in the average living is counted of greatest worth? Is the development of the very best that is possible in us the ruling thought? Is it not rather true that we live to feed, accumulate, and get all the pleasure and profit we can from the world outside of us? The property that we have in ourselves is a nature which is both physical and spiritual. We tend to care more for the animal inheritance than the spiritual. It is tangible, and capable of paying in present pleasure a high rate of interest. I know that in the struggle for existence human life naturally tends to become sordid. This is the evil from which God, in the gospel of our Lord

Jesus Christ, would deliver us. The humblest toiler may, and often does, find a divine purpose in his being, and lives nobly and hopefully through all his toils. We are compelled for our own personal safety to conform to certain moral standards and observe certain outward decencies. Reputation must be preserved and actual crime avoided. We may even stand, like the Pharisee, and thank God that we are not "as other men are, extortioners, unjust, adulterers, or even as this publican." But it is the worth of our reputation that we are thinking of, not the worth of manhood. This is the personal Pharisaism to which we are all liable. When there is an issue made in some moment of secret temptation between the animal and the spiritual, we count the sheep of more value than the man. It is easy to see that men and women may be very respectable outwardly, and scrupulous in the observance of social proprieties, and yet be selfish, sensual, and, in all that constitutes true manhood or womanhood, dead. They may have no sense of the eternal worth and divine capacities of their withered souls, but to justify the indulgence of their lower nature

—to save a sheep—they will strain the elastic standards of society to the point of breaking.

That which is true of the individual pervades, of course, the social world of which he is the unit. That in all our social life a sheep is reckoned of more value than a man— property put before manhood—is a fact so conspicuous that it requires no proof. Society is based upon the security, the distribution, and the accumulation of property. This is a necessity of our material existence. We must get bread and clothing and shelter, but in the universal scramble the desire to accumulate becomes a passion. Differences in ability, education, circumstance, inheritance, create inequalities which clothe some with power over others. That there is something higher to be thought of in our relations to other men than power, place, wealth, or service is an idea which has found but little toleration in the world's history. The worth of manhood at one period has been measured by the conquests which could be achieved by it; at another by the rank, royalty, or other prestige that could be maintained by it; at another by the wealth which it could be made to yield. The world of a later age is beginning to see that there is something better to be considered in our relations to one another than all these—that there is a worth in manhood, gold in the rough ore, which is property of infinitely more value to nations than a sheep. Distrust disintegrates the foundations of society, and the social world is full of strife and envy, because this thought is only dimly perceived and feebly acted upon. There is a Pharisaism in politics which, under a show of patriotism, seeks place and power or party interest; in commercial life which, under those forms of honesty which security demands, often wrongs and corrupts in the haste to be rich; in our social conventions which "pays tithe of mint, anise, and cumin," and forgets, in the daily touch with humanity, purity, justice, mercy, and truth; in religion even, which, having the form of godliness, will sacrifice truth to a system, neglect small charities for big philanthropies, and lose the spirit of Christ in zeal for a prerogative or ecclesiastical tradition or ritual observances. The Pharisee was not wrong in his observances. He stood for the worship of the one God, and was a strict moralist. "These things ought ye to have done," said Christ, "and not to leave the other undone." He was condemned because he was thoroughly egotistical in his observances, and cared more for his pride, prejudice, and property than he did for the chief end of the law— the welfare of men, the worth of manhood.

Now turn from this painful glance at a state of society in which a sheep is counted of more value than a man, and think of the new principle which to the Pharisaism of His own time the Christ opposed when He said, "How much then is a man of more value than a sheep!" The worth of manhood was the supreme thought of His mind and ministry. It was a purely original thought. That mankind in general should be otherwise than hopelessly barbarian never entered into the imagination of the Greek philosopher. Religion before Christ was a cult or a mystery into which only a learned few could enter. I do not forget that Confucius inculcated the social virtues, and that the Buddha taught men to be kind to one another. But there was neither God nor hope in their system. They realised the social value of a sympathetic habit, but of the worth of manhood before God, and its divine capacities, they had no conception. Their teaching lacked force, because it met no sense of a higher destiny than earth, in man. That through and underneath the dark, dreary Alaskan wilderness of a downtrodden humanity there should be wealth of spiritual being more precious than gold, never entered the mind of the old civilisation. Christ came to seek and bring to light the buried manhood, —to purge away its dross, and to build up out of it " Jerusalem the golden."

See how He defied all the prejudices of those haughty Pharisees when He said to the man with the withered hand, " Stretch it forth," and immediately it was restored. Tradition says that the man had been a stone-cutter, whom some form of paralysis had rendered helpless. He may have become a sort of tramp who made capital out of his infirmity. A sheep might have seemed to be of more worth to society than he was; but he was a man,—that was his claim upon our Lord's sympathy. The worth of manhood is opposed to the worth of an animal. It was something to restore him to self-help and usefulness, but that was not all. The

Christ had a deeper purpose in all His healing, helping touch with humanity. That man, so nobly lifted out of the pit of his infirmity and extricated from the net which Pharisaism would have thrown round him, could not quite forget the Healer. It is true that there were ten lepers cleansed, but only one returned to give glory to God. One, however, did return, and he was a Samaritan; but there was an eternal uplifting for him in the gracious words, " Arise, and go thy way: thy faith hath made thee whole." The nine missed the wealth of spiritual blessing which he realised, because they did not act up to the best that was in them and give glory to the power that cleansed them. We do not know what effect Christ's goodness had upon the man with the withered hand, but he never could have forgotten the sympathy which touched and healed him. I do not believe he could have been among the mob which cried out, " Let Him be crucified!" His life must have been different and nobler from the hour that he met Jesus Christ. But whatever may have been his subsequent history, we know that our Lord by His sympathy lifted the Samaritan leper up to a higher life; that He opened the blind eyes of Bartimeus, whom the Pharisees cast out, to the vision of a new and immortal life through faith; that He brought down Zaccheus, the despised publican, from his leafy hiding-place, and by recognising the better spirit that was latent in him made a new man of him; and that He drew the Magdalene to His feet in loving devotion, for ever purified by His pardoning word. It was not men's bodies that He was seeking to save, but their souls, through their bodies. How pathetically this was shown in the sad refrain to the cleansing of the lepers: "Were there not ten cleansed? but where are the nine?" It was to lead out men's spiritual nature that He was working. This was education in its highest sense. He saw in the rough fishermen and many a despised publican and miserable outcast such value before God that when one of them repented He declared that there was joy in heaven.

But what was it that gave such worth to manhood? The Christ was the merchant of His own parable, who, having found one pearl of great price, went and sold all that he had and bought it. But what is the pearl that was worthy of the price which Christ paid for it, even the giving of Himself to live, suffer, and die in the flesh? He has Himself defined it in the familiar words as they are rendered by St. Luke: "What is a man profited, if he gain the whole world, and lose or forfeit his own self?" The self in us which lies back of the animal self, and which is capable of receiving and knowing the Father of our spirits and partaking of His own eternal life, is the "pearl of great price"— the "treasure hid in a field"—the lost son who, "when he *came to himself*," said, "I will arise and go to my father." Through all Christ's work and teaching we find Him seeking this spiritual self in mankind, which was lost under the darkness of an earthly, sensual habit. It could be satisfied only with God, and therefore every soul which had not made darkness its element was responsive to Him. He could not reach the Pharisees, because they had buried their true spiritual selves beneath the form of religion itself, and, while they seemed to be religious, were only gorgeous sepulchres, full of pride and selfishness. The habit of self-seeking, of reckoning even in their religion the sheep of more value than man, had so incrusted them that they had no life left in them. There were others in whom the rank overgrowth of fleshly thoughts and habits had completely choked the growth of a higher self. It has been so in every age. There are respectable men and women now who are so incased in the pride of their own opinions and moral and intellectual sufficiency that only a resurrection from the dead could restore them to life and light. There seems to be also a large class so completely brutalised that we can only think of the Master's own words when we try to reach them: "Give not that which is holy unto the dogs, neither cast ye your pearls before swine, lest they trample them under their feet, and turn again and rend you." But by every means He sought to waken men to the consciousness of the divine possibilities that were in them. When He drew the fisher disciples to Himself, and made them His apostles, this was the charge: "Come ye after me, and I will make you fishers of men." This was to be the mission of their lives and of the whole church. The love of Christ, seeking goodly pearls, found in Saul of Tarsus, a Pharisee, and the son of Pharisees, that pearl of great price, the splendid manhood of Paul the Apostle. This was the experience through which the Pharisaism of Saul was transmuted into the glowing Christian character of Paul: "When it pleased God to reveal His Son in me, immediately I conferred not with flesh and blood." He was a new man—old things had passed away—the moment that he realised in deepest penitence "how much a man is of more value than a sheep."

I have spoken of the general tendency of the world's thought to reckon a sheep of more value than a man, and then of the supreme purpose of the Christ to reverse this false estimate and make us know that a man is of more value than a sheep. I ask you to think, in conclusion, of the immense practical importance in its bearing upon our individual and social welfare of Christ's estimate of manhood.

We are not animals. We are men. The effort to prove that we are only animal has failed. Science itself is groping among the infinities, and has to recognise a "supreme moment in man's history when the psychical began to dominate the physical." The life of many men is, indeed, so completely subject to the physical that the sheep puts them to shame. The sheep lives out its own quiet nature; but they are not living true to themselves. The sheep is content to graze; but they are not content. They often loathe themselves. The disgust, the shame, the remorse, prove that they are capable of something higher. The very fierceness of men's passions is evidence that they are more than animals. The natural brute beast, in obeying its instincts, does not prey upon itself; but a man does. He makes a ruin of his body, because he violates the laws of his being. The voluptuary, the drunkard, the glutton, all sin against themselves. The laws of our being must, therefore, demand a higher service than that of the bodily appetites. We are capable not only of that mental development which we call education, and which enables man to dominate the earth, but of a spiritual development which makes for godlikeness in character. This is the worth of manhood, that, knowing God in Jesus Christ, we may open our true spiritual selves in faith to His love, and realise that He is our Father in the same high sense that He was the Father of our Lord Jesus Christ. It is through the knowledge of God, you perceive, and the realisation by faith of our undying sonship with Him, that we find the worth of manhood. Christianity offers the individual man a better hope than wheeling through endless cycles of change, and then, if he has kept the " right rules," the blessedness of " ceasing to be," as

"The dewdrop slips into the shining sea."

It does not find his ultimate destiny in that Nirvana where, as a certain poet describes it,

"Seeking nothing, he gains all;
Foregoing self, the universe grows 'I.'"

God, the eternal Father, stands for " I " in the Christian faith. He is a present God, shining in the face of the incarnate Jesus, imaged in our pure human loves and relationships, dwelling in our hearts, if we will, by faith. To " walk in the light, as He is in the light," not by an ascetic denial or denouncing of the flesh, nor despising the common life of men, nor separating ourselves from the every-day business of the world, but by living up to the best that is in us, keeping ourselves open to God, and our bodies in subjection, and carrying brightness, hope, patience, and goodness into all our touch with the present world—this is the manhood and womanhood of which we are capable.

> "The sweet persuasion of His voice
> Respects thy sanctity of will:
> He giveth day; thou hast thy choice
> To walk in darkness still."

The social worth of men and women who walk in the God-given day cannot be overestimated. There is certainly no property of more real value to the world than virtuous manhood and womanhood. There are no principles which more surely tend to evolve the highest virtue than the principles of love to God and man. Christianity is the only religion which has been able to realise them in human lives and make them living forces in our civilisation. What nobler use, then, can we make of ourselves in this brief life of ours than so to live that the world shall be the richer for our being? We may acquire material wealth and bless the world with it, but there is a wealth of Christian character which is capital of infinitely more value to the world than gold. It is a splendid thing when character and gold are united in one man; but, comparatively speaking, sterling character is worth vastly more than sterling gold. No large philanthropies or generous bequests will condone for unworthy living. The world needs the best coinage of your manhood and your womanhood, and you are responsible for its awful poverty of being if you do not give it gold bearing the image and superscription, not of Cæsar, but of God.

And what beautiful new lights are thrown upon the missionary idea when we look at it from the Christ's point of view! St. Paul wrote to the Corinthian Christians: "I seek not yours, but you." This is the true missionary idea. It has in view the worth of manhood to God, to society, and to itself, and not exclusively that which has complicated the whole question of missions—salvation from some impending doom hereafter. Men are property of more value than sheep, and therefore, to lead them up to the highest and best that is possible is certainly a splendid work, both in its present and its eternal results. If He who gave Himself for us rejoiced and the angels in heaven echoed His joy, over one sinner that repenteth, surely we who call ourselves Christians ought wherever we touch men in our families and business and by every other opportunity, to seek to lift them up to the life which God their Father would have them live. The world needs this nobler estimate of the worth of manhood. When there is a great enthusiasm for it we shall have not only the solving of many of our problems, but the incoming of the promised kingdom of God among men.

I have been able only to suggest thoughts which are worthy of your more careful consideration. There is hope for a soul that has not died down beneath the experience which is described in St. Paul's words: "The good that I would, I do not: but the evil which I would not, that I do. . . . O wretched man that I am! who shall deliver me from the body of this death?" Turning to God in the faith of His love, sealed by the precious blood of Christ, abiding in the communion of His Church, and walking in love, as Christ also loved us, that soul may reckon itself dead indeed unto sin, but alive unto God, through Jesus Christ our Lord.

There are men and women, not only in the slums but in the best circles of society, who, like Cleopatra, in the very wantonness of luxury dissolve pearls in their wine-cup and drink them; not the perishable pearls of earth, but their own spiritual selves which Christ came to redeem, and which He would set in the crown of His glory to shine like the stars for ever and ever. They hold the golden chalice of life in their hands, but not content to drink and be thankful for that which God gives, they put the pearl of great price into it and dissolve it away in mere frivolity.

While you have life, and quickly, before death strikes the golden cup from your grasp, give yourselves to God, in the faith of Christ, in the communion of His Church, in nobleness of living; and so shall you be numbered with those blessed ones of whom it is written, "They shall be mine, saith the Lord, in that day when I make up my jewels."

XII.

The Everlasting Possession.

7.

XII.

THE EVERLASTING POSSESSION.

And I will give unto thee, and to thy seed after thee, the land wherein thou art a stranger, all the land of Canaan, for an everlasting possession; and I will be their God.—GEN. xvii. 8.

THIS was God's promise to Abraham. Notice the terms of the promise: "Unto thee"—not "to thy seed" only, but "unto thee"—will I give "all the land of Canaan," and that for an "everlasting possession."

Now the peculiar fact is that the terms were not realised, either for him or for his seed. He wandered as a stranger in the land of Canaan. He never inherited it. The only possession he really had in it was the possession of a burial-place, which he purchased. His posterity, after the bondage in Egypt and the weary wandering in the wilderness, ultimately subdued the Canaanites; but they found no everlasting possession. They were temporarily established under David and Solomon; but the glory of the Jewish kingdom soon faded, and they were carried into captivity and the land overrun with strangers. They never thoroughly rallied again. The Promised Land is profaned by strangers again to-day, and those to whom it was given as an everlasting possession are scattered abroad. Was Abraham the victim of a cruel deception? Did he go out from his own land, not knowing whither he went, and dwell in tents, and endure hardships, led by no brighter hope than the possible glory of his posterity in the far-off future—a glory which he was not to witness? Was there no hope for the patriarch beyond the tomb which was his only possession and his only resting-place in time? "I will give unto thee the land wherein thou art a stranger;"—but he died a stranger in it. Where, then, was the fulfilment?

The New Testament throws light upon the question. Stephen recognised the strange fact in his address before the council, when he said, speaking of Abraham, " God removed him into this land, wherein ye now dwell. And He gave him none inheritance in it, no, not so much as to set his foot on: yet He promised that He would give it to him for a possession, and to his seed after him, when as yet he had no child." Our Lord relieves the difficulty which the patriarch's death seemed to interpose, by teaching us that the God who is called the God of Abraham, and the God of Isaac, and the God of Jacob, is not a God of the dead, but "of the living"; for "all live unto Him." The resurrection may accomplish for Abraham that which his death seemed to forbid. He has not passed out of the sphere of God's covenant mercy. He has not ceased to be. He may still inherit.

The author of the Epistle to the Hebrews shows us that this future realisation of the promise is not only possible, but that to it Abraham looked. Through the fading of his earthly hope he saw rising into view a better, even a heavenly, country. "By faith" he went out "into a place which he should after receive for an inheritance, . . . not knowing whither he went. By faith he became a sojourner in the land of promise, as in a land not his own, dwelling in tents, with Isaac and Jacob, the heirs with him of the same promise." By faith he was able to see the earthly promise fail, because he "looked for the city which hath the foundations, whose builder and maker is God." The same strong faith, you perceive, which at God's command would have offered up Isaac, accounting that God was able to raise him up even from the dead, enabled him to look through the temporal Canaan to the eternal inheritance of which it was only the shadow and the preparation.

It is clear, then, that the promise is yet to be fulfilled. Abraham waits for it; his posterity wait for it. "These all," says the apostle, "died in faith, not having received the promises, but having seen them and greeted them from afar, and having confessed that they were strangers and pilgrims on the earth." But who are Abraham's children? Are they the circumcision only? Not the circumcision only, but the uncircumcision also. "For," says St. Paul, "if ye are Christ's, then are ye Abraham's seed, heirs according to promise." Believers stand therefore where Abraham stood, not having received the promises but "greeting them from afar." There is wealth of suggestion in these facts.

They help us to understand life's failure—to realise our hopes—the relation of the temporal to the eternal, and the office of faith in a changing world.

We need not labour to prove that *the present life does not realise the promises of God to us and in us.* I say "in us" as well as "to us," because every man has intuitions of enjoyment, honour, and immortality which he expects life to realise. They are born with him, and as clearly prophesy of the things they crave as hunger and thirst prophesy of food and drink. But the earthly Canaan does not satisfy these prophetic cravings. The most prosperous find at last only a burial-place. Their possessions pass to others. The world is no everlasting possession. We long for immortality, but we do not find it here. "The things which are seen are temporal." The promises which are written on our hearts are reaffirmed by the Word of God. The present does not satisfy, and yet we are told that the meek-spirited shall possess the earth and shall be refreshed in the multitude of peace. "The kingdom and dominion, and the greatness of the kingdom under the whole heaven," says Daniel,

" shall be given to the people of the saints of the Most High, whose kingdom is an everlasting kingdom." Christ reiterates the promise, declaring: "Blessed are the meek: for they shall inherit the earth." "All things are yours," cries the apostle; "whether . . . the world, or life, or death, or things present, or things to come." Is the world ours? Do the saints possess it? Generation after generation has passed away, realising little more in the visible present than conflict, temptation, and martyrs' graves. God's people do not, certainly, rule the earth. It is largely in the hands of those who are foreign to God. They are strangers in it. They dwell in tents, like Abraham and his children. They see the "wicked in great power, and flourishing like a green bay-tree," while they more often inherit poverty and pain than prosperity. They die and turn again to their dust, like other men, and then all their thoughts seem to perish. The earth which they are to inherit yields them, in brief, no rest for their souls, no permanent joy, no sure, unchanging foundation for their hopes, no immortality of life and love. Their chief experience in the present is the experience of life's fickleness, uncertainty, and weariness. They confess, with the patriarchs, that they are "pilgrims and strangers on the earth." Well said Paul: "If in this life only we have hope in Christ, we are of all men most miserable." If His promise means nothing more than the inheritance which we have in this present life, then we are cruelly deceived;— for His will brings us into conflict with the flesh, makes the world unfriendly to us, and yields us no brighter hope than the possible supremacy of the Christian Church in the far-off future — no richer compensation than the sense of having sacrificed ourselves and crucified our earthly desires for the possession of a burial-place in which life and its unfulfilled promises must be buried together.

It is clear that for us, as for Abraham, the present does not exhaust the promises of God. We must look for their fulfilment to that regenerated earth into which the resurrection shall usher all who have died in the faith, from Adam and Abel and Enoch to the latest saint over whom mourners weep. But are we to ignore and despise the present? Has it no relation to the eternal? Is it only illusory and obstructive?

These questions bring us to our second point: *the relation of the temporal to the eternal.* Life's failure to realise our hopes may be variously interpreted. Some adopt the Epicurean interpretation of the mystery: " Let us eat, drink, and be merry to-day: for to-morrow we die." Get all the good you can out of the present; save what you can from the wreck. The ship is sinking; the ocean of oblivion will soon swallow you up. All the possibilities of pleasure perish in the grave; revel and riot while you may.

Others run to the opposite extreme and adopt the ascetic view of life. Ignore, they say, the present, with its relations, associations, and pursuits, altogether; they are essentially hostile to God and the Christian life. Withdraw into the cloister; put on sackcloth, crucify every affection which looks earthward, and spend your time in meditation and prayer. The one view proceeds upon the assumption that there is no promise beyond the temporal; the other assumes that the promise is altogether beyond and independent of the temporal.

The truth, as usual, lies between the two extremes. We are to realise the promise, not in the temporal, nor apart from it, but *through* it. The earthly Canaan was the image of the heavenly inheritance. Abraham was led out through it into the knowledge of God and dependence upon Him. His pilgrim experience strengthened his faith, and through the fading of the earthly promise he gained a clearer vision of the eternal things beyond. So his posterity found a wilderness on the other side of the Red Sea; but they entered into a closer acquaintance with God and His will and providential care. When the land flowing with milk and honey was reached, they had to encounter many foes and painful vicissitudes; but they found a Temple, with its prophetic sacrifices and eloquent types pointing on to a Redeemer and His better kingdom. When, at a later period, their land sank away from them and they were submerged in captivity to a strange people, they heard the voices of the prophets and saw through the gloom the golden walls of "the city which hath the foundations." And when, again, they were under the Roman yoke, and literally strangers in their own land, Christ arose upon their view, a "bright and morning star" to all who looked for the consolation of Israel, heralding a new day of spiritual life and light and glory. Their temporal experiences were like a series of dissolving views, each one fading into some brighter vision; and still the people of God are looking through all the changes and chances of this mortal life for brighter things to come. The earthly Canaan was their school-room, in which they were taught by object-lessons to know God, and trained for that nobler citizenship which awaited them.

Now, precisely that is the relation of the things seen and temporal to "the things unseen and eternal." They are neither to be idolised as if they were ends of being, nor ignored as if they were necessarily evil, but to be used as means of knowing God, and as affording a discipline or education for the higher, freer life to come. If you consider the present world in this view, as the school-room in which we may be taught and disciplined for eternity, I think you will see that the temporal things have their proper and blessed uses. They are the picture-forms in which eternal truths are made known to us as they could not be known otherwise. Creation, in its manifold hues and shapes, gives expression to the invisible power within. We may read the divine wisdom, might, and love in it, just as we read the emotions of a human soul in the features of the living face. We are drawn out of ourselves to seek the invisible forces which play through the material world in the light and growth and beauty which our eyes witness everywhere. Not in the realms of abstract thought does the child or the man learn of God, but through the creation which witnesses of the Creator. If some will not heed the voices which would lead them on to the sanctuary of God's presence, the fault is not in His world, but in their deaf ears, which will hear nothing but the movement of a vast machine in the measured roll of the universe. Christ's Incarnation is the crowning evidence of God's purpose to teach us "the invisible things . . . through the things that are made."

The daily ministries also of the world outside of us are constantly bringing near to us the Providence by which we are sustained. The daily bread is a perpetual sign of the divine presence. The farmer sows the seed, but he cannot control the unseen power which crowns the seed with the abundant harvest. The products of our industry are all gathered out of invisible hands. Let a man look through them to the power which gives the increase, and he will find himself in communion with a God who cares for his soul as well as his body. He will find in the law of material growth the law of spiritual life. He will be able to understand the logic of our Lord's saying, when He drew (as He so often did) lessons from nature: "If God so clothe the grass of the field, which to-day is, and to-morrow is cast into the oven, how much more shall He clothe you, O ye of little faith!" and the deep significance of that other saying: "Whatsoever a man soweth, that shall he also reap."

And so, too, the various relations of life are the shadows of divine realities. Viewed, not as permanent forms, but as the figures of something higher, holier, truer, they are full of meaning. The child learns in the family the authority of law administered in love. The parent is taught the sacredness of that childish trust which none but a fiend would betray, and he may know from what his child is to him what he may be to God. Fatherhood and motherhood are but feeble types of that which is possible in the great Father towards those who trust Him. Marriage reflects the mystical union of Christ and His Church, and brotherhood is the image of the heavenly society. If we merely look at the forms of our temporal life, and see no happiness beyond them, we must be sorely disappointed when they fade away, as fade they must. But when we look through them to the eternal life, in which they are to be glorified and immortalised, we know how to use them wisely, and secure for them, by Christianising them, a permanence which they could not have on earth.

But not only do things temporal shadow forth divine truths; they form, in their grouping around each life, a discipline which develops character and educates us for the heavenly inheritance. They are for ever changing, and to those who look for an earthly Canaan life's racking disappointments, and shifting fortunes, and desolating sorrows seem to make it a vast wilderness. They dream of a paradise which they never find. They try to make for themselves a resting-place,—as Lot did when he pitched his tent towards Sodom,—but God drives them out by some fiery providence which consumes their hopes, and would in mercy teach them that this is not their rest. But to those who see in the earthly Canaan only a preparation for the heavenly, life's changes are ordered in God's providence for a blessed purpose. The kaleidoscope reveals only darkness and confusion to one who will not look through it to the light; but when the light streams in, each turn of the glass reveals some new form of beauty. When we look through the present to eternity, and see that present in the light of heavenly promise, each turn of the glass, though it may throw our plans into confusion, and break up our earthly hopes, and desolate our home circle, yet discloses some new and blessed experience. Through the wasting of our material wealth we realise in our souls a better and more enduring substance. Through the cares and conflicts and disappointments of each year we see more of the Saviour's preciousness and power. Through the bereavements which spoil our earthly attachments we enter into brighter experiences of heaven's reality and love. Faith sees, when the tears are wiped away, that all things are working together for good.

Faith, you perceive, is the realising and sustaining power in this changing world. This is its high office. It has well been called the " substance of things hoped for, the evidence of things not seen." It is faith which sees the heavenly Canaan reflected in the earthly. It is faith which opens the door of the ark, and bids hope spread its wings, like the dove, and bring back some olive-leaf plucked off, to cheer the imprisoned soul and assure it of the rest beyond. It is faith which glorifies the present with the spirit of the invisible, and makes us content to be pilgrims and strangers on the earth. It is faith which pierces the angriest storm-cloud and sings like a bird in the upper heavens while the lightnings play below. It is faith which, like the man at the masthead looking over the fog and guiding the ship by that which is unseen to those below, steers a straight course into the peaceful harbour.

If you would realise the joy of being, you

must walk by faith, not by sight. Those who walk by sight only, believing nothing which their senses cannot perceive, make the world their dungeon. Their noblest faculties wither in the gloom, and though they may revel for a little, the walls close round them and the dungeon becomes their tomb. The eyes of the soul are darkened, and they see only the bare, cold walls of their dwelling. Faith is the soul's second sight; it sees, through the earthly and the temporal, things unseen and eternal. It is not a sickly sentiment, opposed to the practical and exercised apart from the common life. It sees a beauty in nature, and breathes in an exhilaration from the everlasting hills which the unbeliever knows not. It finds a meaning in the pure relations of life, and gleans lessons from them, which make them ever sacred. It dignifies the commonest task, and enables the man in his counting-house or at the bench to do immortal work by doing all to the glory of God. It reveals to the mourner a Saviour in every sorrow, and down through the years of our pilgrimage, and beyond the burial-place which awaits every one of us, it discloses the better country, the land which is to be our everlasting possession—the pearly gates of the New Jerusalem.

Learn, then, as you look into the shadowy future stretching away before you, how to use the present life. Don't rest your hopes upon it; don't seek satisfaction from it; don't expect permanency in it. Some of us who cherish high hopes now may before another dawn have found only the possession of a burial-place. But while we would not have you rest in and idolise the temporal, we would have you look through it into the divine life which it shadows forth,—recognising the royal Giver in His gifts, and honouring Him in their use,—entering into the eternal society of which the home circle is the transient image,—heeding the duties which press upon you in your business as duties which He commands,—accepting the trials which meet you as stern but merciful preceptors,—and developing through all life's changes faith, hope, patience, charity,—in a word, the character which shall qualify you for that higher life when we shall have put off the masks of the flesh and stand as we really are before our God.

XIII.

"My Lord and My God."

XIII.

"MY LORD AND MY GOD."

Thomas answered and said unto Him, My Lord and my God.—ST. JOHN xx. 28.

THOMAS stood in the presence of the risen Christ. The other disciples had told him, "We have seen the Lord." Doubting, he had replied: "Except I shall see in His hands the print of the nails, and put my finger into the print of the nails, and thrust my hand into His side, I will not believe." The Christ now offered to him sensible proof—the scarred hands and side. But doubt vanished like a flash. There was something in that presence that wrought instantaneous conviction. He seems not to have accepted the proffered test of reality. He was convinced of the fact that Christ had risen from the dead, and more,—much more,—he realised in the profoundest depths of his feeling, as by a sudden revelation, all that the fact meant for him personally. He gives us the fullest confession of faith that had yet been made by any of the disciples: "My Lord and my God." This confession has peculiar interest for us, because it stands midway between the faith of the disciples before the resurrection and that which afterwards united them in a closer spiritual relation to their Lord. It is the very full expression of that which must unite us to a risen and living Lord, "He that liveth, and was dead; and behold, He is alive for evermore." But Thomas stood in the *presence* of his Lord. He *saw* and believed. How then can his faith be taken as the standard of the faith to which we are called? Our Lord, anticipating the period of His absence in which we live, adds the saying, "Because thou hast seen me, thou hast believed: blessed are they that have not seen, and yet have believed." It is possible, then, for us to stand in his relation of absolute, personal, glad conviction, "not having seen." Let us seek to understand how this may be.

Thomas believed because he saw; but that which he saw was *not the whole of that which he believed.* That which he saw was the ground of a faith in something which he did not see with the bodily eyes. His confession was not the cold assent of an intellect convinced of a fact about Christ by sensible proof. He did not look at the scars and say: "I am convinced that the stories are true, and that you have actually risen from the dead." He looked through this fact to the glory of the divine Person which —as in a burst of light—it revealed to him. It was not the reason only, but warm spiritual affections and perceptions, which spoke in the exclamation, "My Lord and my God." That which he saw through the veil of a visible presence remains to us. It is true that the person of Christ is only known to us through certain authentic records, compiled by persons who lived and walked with Him on earth more than eighteen hundred years ago. Those ancient records stand in the place of that bodily form which Thomas saw. I am disposed, however, to think that the proof of Christ's having lived, died, and risen again is quite as strong for us in them as the sensible proof was for Thomas. If Christ had continued to manifest Himself visibly on the earth as He did to Thomas, the critics, who have no moral sympathy with nor capability of perceiving the meaning of the fact, would still find reason to discredit the evidence of their senses, as they do the historic testimony,— "Neither would they be persuaded, though one rose from the dead." We have the written records. We may look at them with the cold, critical gaze of the intellect, and find abundant evidence that such a man as Jesus Christ really lived, suffered, died, and even rose again. We may accept the evidence, but He will only be to us as any other historic character of the past. We shall have accepted certain facts about Christ, but fall very far short of the faith of Thomas. We shall be just where he would have been if, accepting the sensible proofs of Christ's having risen, he had believed the fact, and failed to perceive and receive the divine personality which it disclosed to him. There are many who feel the wisdom of Christ's teaching and the power of His example; but they never get beyond this. They are like persons who have no soul to feel the power of the masterpiece of sculpture or of painting. A Raphael's "Madonna" is only to them a mass of coloring, or the "Apollo" a skilfully carved stone. The genius, the feeling, the thought, which live in these works, they have no capacity to appreciate. They miss entirely the beauty, enjoyment, and living power of works of genius.

There is within the external facts of the gospel, or rather shining out through them, a beauty of *moral character* which has made itself felt and been a convincing power in every age. Every man who is alive in his perceptions to the attractions of goodness, purity, and truth is compelled to reverence the character of Christ. We have a most striking illustration of this fact in the language of one of the leaders of that movement towards religious reform which has made memorable in India the last half-century. " Our business," he writes, " is with the spiritual, universal, and living Christ. Not the Son of man, but the Son of God, in Christ, is needful for our salvation. In the purely human Christ we can hardly feel any interest; but the divine elements of His character come home to every man's bosom and business, and are of the highest importance to our redemption as involving the eternal and universal principles of ethics.

He does not come to us as God, the Father, Ruler, and Saviour, in human form; nor is He to us a mere good man who lived a pious life and died a noble death. He stands before us always as the incarnation of faith and loyalty to God, an example of self-sacrificing devotion to truth. He is to be accepted in spirit, and converted into an internal fact of our life. He is to live in us perpetually as the spirit of godliness. We do not care to believe in an outward and dead Nazarene; but we do care to assimilate the Spirit of Christ to our souls. Thus the Spirit of Christ shall constantly abide in us as the living Christ!" Such was the power of Christ over a mind struggling honestly through the darkest prejudice towards moral truth; interesting because showing how powerful the personality of Christ is, and how it emerges from the historic facts, and how men who love righteousness perceive and feel its influence. "Having not seen, they have in some sort believed."

But this perception of moral beauty and power in Him still falls short of that full perception of the truth which Thomas reached. Keshub Chunder Sen, and others like him, who reverence

Christ as the great Master in righteousness, stand where the believing disciples did before His resurrection. They called Him, with an ever-deepening reverence, "Master and Lord." They were awed by something in Him which was more than human, and which made even the emissaries of His foes turn back from Him abashed, saying: "Never man spake like this man." But they did not perceive the real truth of His personality. It vaguely dawned upon some of them, but not as a full realisation. They caught glimpses of the truth through the correspondence of His mighty works with His more than human character. When He subdued the storm, they cried out: "What manner of man is this, that even the winds and the sea obey Him?"—but that the Man was God they did not then see. It was not until they stood in the presence of the risen Lord that the full meaning of His words, in answer to Philip's demand, "Show us the Father," was realised. "Have I been so long time with you, and yet hast thou not known me, Philip? he that hath seen me hath seen the Father." Here Thomas stood; Christ had been a long time with him, and yet he had not known Him: now he knew Him. The fact of the resurrection was not so much a proof of his Lord's divinity as it was a disclosure of the divinity, which Thomas had but dimly suspected in all his intercourse with that sinless life on earth.

That which he perceived in the fulness of its power, we too may see and feel and adore. In the fact of the resurrection we have a confirmation and full revelation of the truth of Christ's person. The moral beauty of His character is defective without it. If we leave out this fact, and look at Him only through the ordinary human conditions of His life, He may be to us an ideal character; but the ideal is in our imagination; the imagination is not a faithful reflection of the original.—He claimed to be that which He was not; He said that He would rise from the dead, and He did not; His word cannot be trusted, for events falsified it; His proposed work of redemption failed; He is at best only a memory, which has no power to realise in us the life which He promised to impart. It may be said that He "lives" as all great men live—by the force of their example or influence; but the expression is only a rhetorical trope: He does not live for us, personally and potentially. Here is the defect in all those partial views of Christ which see in Him only the supremely good man, and not the risen, living "Lord of all." There is no bridge across the gulf which yawns between our incapacity and the ideal. The Hindoo reformer to whom we have referred saw in Christ an impersonation of faith, love, righteousness, and sacrifice which is to be accepted in spirit and "converted into an internal fact of our life"; but we are left to do the converting part ourselves, which is just that which we cannot do. It is just at this point that we need a Saviour. Herein resides the peculiar distinction of Christianity over every other religious system. It contains within itself the converting forces. "We all, with unveiled face reflecting as a mirror the glory of the Lord, are transformed into the same image from glory to glory."

The resurrection explains and accounts for the transformations of character which have singularly marked the progress of Christianity. It discloses to us in the perfect Lord " the mighty

God, the everlasting Father." It is not so much a proof of Christ's divinity as the necessary and natural manifestation of it. If we look only at the alleged fact we are staggered, perhaps, by the phenomenal event of a man who had died, rising again. But when we look through the fact to the Person who rose, the difficulties vanish; the mystery of the human life is solved; the resurrection becomes a revelation; it clears up all that was strange in His character, words, deeds, and promises. The whole truth flashes upon us, and finds expression in Thomas's words: "My Lord and my God."

This, then, is the faith to which we are called and by which we may realise power. It is the faith of personal trust in a living, though unseen, Christ. He lives for us, as our representative before high Heaven, and in us, if we will, by the power and presence of the Holy Spirit. Not a dead hero, nor a reminiscence, nor an inspiring example merely, but the divine Saviour, living in all the tenderness of that unwearying love, the breadth and depth of that sympathy, the sovereignty of that wisdom, the patience of that saving purpose, the majesty of that truth, righteousness, and redeeming power, which appeared in all His lowly walk among the poor, the sick, the sad, and the sin-burdened on earth. We know about Him through the written records. The critical evidence is important for our understandings, but He was certainly never evolved from the Jewish consciousness of the writers. He is manifestly above them and earth and time. We see Him alive from the dead, risen, glorified, evidently alive for evermore. We are carried out of the historic records. He vanishes out of our sight. We know Him now no more in time, but we are for ever in communion with the unseen and eternal, for God was in Christ. He has not left us comfortless. He is with us, by His Holy Spirit, ruling, teaching, helping, enlightening, purifying—" Jesus Christ, the same yesterday, to-day, and for ever."

I have tried to show you that the glory which Thomas saw in the risen Saviour may be quite as close and real and living for us as for him, because it is the glory of God in the face of Jesus Christ. The blessedness of the relation in which Thomas stood may be ours, through faith, though we see Him not. But observe how *intensely personal* his faith was. He did not say, "Thou art indeed the Lord and God," but—like a child lost in a dark, bewildering forest, who suddenly recognises in the shadowy form approaching him his own seeking father — he exclaimed: "*My* Lord and *my* God." Christ was never after that a character of the past to him, nor an absent Saviour. He vanished out of his sight, but He was still a living reality to him, in the same experience of faith as that which St. Peter describes as the experience of all believers, One " whom having not seen ye love; in whom, though now ye see Him not, yet believing, ye rejoice with joy unspeakable and full of glory: receiving the end of your faith, even the salvation of your souls."

Christ must be known in such an experience of personal revelation and personal surrender, or He remains outside of us and we remain unblessed. Do not suppose that He is a sort of bartering Lord, who demands a certain quality or degree of faith as a condition of His favour. It is simply that no faith which is not personal trust is really faith in Him at all. It may be an historic or propositional faith about Him; but that differs as widely from trust on Him as belief in the system of medicine which your physician practises differs from confiding yourself to him and taking his medicine when you are sick. Personal trust realises power, because it is a yielding to Christ in all that He is, and would be, to us. He stands at the door and knocks. If any of you are not blessed, it is because you will not let Him come in. You will not yield to Him as your sovereign Lord, and therefore He is not in you the power of God unto salvation. You oppose your will to Him at some point. He cannot be Lord and God to you if you have other gods than Him. The gods of your ambition, your profit, your pleasure, your pride, must be cast down. Doubt need not stand in the way. Honest doubt will perceive, through the shadow, that to walk as Christ walked is the true righteousness. Accepting this truth, and doing it, the doubter will soon emerge from his darkness, as Thomas did, and confess Christ "Lord and God." But there must be self-surrender. "He that will save his life"—his present, earthly, selfish life—"shall lose life"; and he that "will lose his life"—his self-life—for Christ's sake shall find the true life. That is the law of Christ's kingdom. The trouble with many of us is that we do not trust Him enough to risk the present loss and give up our poor scheme of life. We are not willing, for His sake,—for the sake of the righteousness, the goodness, the eternal glory, which He represents,—to let the present indulgences, the possible realisation of our delusive dreams, go. The trust which dares to do it, in a full surrender, realises the abiding presence and power of a living Christ. "I am crucified with Christ," said St. Paul; "nevertheless I live; and yet not I, but Christ liveth in me." That was a real experience for him. It may be real in us. Knowing Him as a living presence with our spirit, we know the Father.

Do we not need above all things, in this dark world, to find and know our God? He is not far from every one of us. Let me tell you where you may meet Him. Back of that physical existence which you share with the brute creatures, and back, too, of that which you call your outward life, with its relations and obligations and business, there is the hidden, secret life of the soul. Here the "you," the true self, lives and broods and knows itself as the world cannot know it. Here every man is alone; and it is an awful, gloomy solitariness to many. They can find nothing better to do in life than to seek diversion—something which will make them forget themselves. Here, in this silent, lonely chamber of your self-consciousness, every one of you has at some time felt the brooding, awful mystery of life. The sense of yourself, and the awful loneliness of your being, as of one lost under the midnight dreariness of an arctic sea, has oppressed you. Here every one of you has felt at times a longing to be something better than he is. You have felt the shame of your mean, low, selfish lives. The vision of something higher and nobler has passed before you, and you have aspired and resolved; but the chains of earthly habit have been too strong for you. Here, when your lives have been made desolate and your hearts tempest-tossed with grief, you have longed for some rift in the overhanging clouds, some light to shine through from the unseen world, some glimpse of stars in the deep, voiceless azure of immensity, to save you from utter despair. It is here, upon the threshold of this inner room of our being, a room which opens towards the infinities, that God, in Christ, waits to reveal Himself. You have felt Him here, every one of you, though perhaps you knew Him not, pleading with you to turn from your sin and selfishness and yield yourselves to Him and His service. You have gone out from this presence, this pleading of your better nature, and tried to forget it amid the excitements of the world. Oh, to give up resistance and in the silence and secrecy of your soul to confess your need and sin and weakness, to see in His wounded hands and side the pledges of the Father's pardoning love, to "let the light of the knowledge of the glory of God in the face of Jesus Christ" shine in your heart, to look into that face with an absorbing devotion and a self-surrendering trust, saying in all the testimony of your life, as well as of your lips, "My Lord and my God"!—this is life eternal, for it is to know God, and Jesus Christ, whom He hath sent. Knowing Jesus, you know the Father. Trusting Him, God is your Father. Yielding to Him in the obedience of love, you make way for God to take possession of you and to save you. Living out of yourself in self-devotion to Christ, you live in a new world of fellowships, relations, and sympathies; you live above the present, in the communion of the unseen and eternal. Drawn out of your own selfishness to Christ, and to God in Christ, you have found the true life for man.

XIV.

Other Men's Labours.

XIV.

OTHER MEN'S LABOURS.

And herein is that saying true, One soweth, and another reapeth. I sent you to reap that whereon ye bestowed no labour: other men laboured, and ye are entered into their labours.—St. JOHN iv. 37, 38.

OUR Lord had been talking with the Samaritan woman. She was, you remember, at first flippant, then interested, then serious, and then so thoroughly aroused that she left the vessel which she had brought to the well, and hurried back to the Samaritan town to bid her fellow-citizens, "Come, see a man, which told me all things that ever I did: is not this the Christ?" Meantime the disciples, who had gone into the town to buy food, returned, and urged Him to eat. But He answered: "My meat is to do the will of Him that sent me, and to finish His work." The ardour of His soul for God and truth consumed every lower feeling and lifted Him out of the low range of bodily necessities. The return of the disciples suggested their part in the joy which filled His own soul. He was reluctant to leave the pure heights in which His mind was ranging, and descend to ordinary things. The budding fields were spread out, rich with promise, before Him. Beyond them was the Samaritan town. He saw the people, stirred by the woman's words, hastening towards Him. Still dreaming of the spiritual, He gathers up a figure from the fields and travels quickly on with it to the approaching multitude: "Say not ye, There are yet four months, and then cometh harvest? behold, I say unto you, Lift up your eyes, and look on the fields, for they are white already to the harvest." "See how quickly the seed ripens. The soil is ready for it. The Spirit of God attends it. Already these people come to see and inquire." This, He goes on to show, is a field worth toiling in. He was the sower who went forth to sow. The disciples were to be the reapers. Sure and happy, He would have them know, would be the reapers' work. "He that reapeth receiveth wages," or a reward. You shall have, He means, a present joy, a real satisfaction, a continual blessing, in doing the work, but in the results of that ministry there shall be a still richer compensation. The spiritual reaper gathereth fruit unto life eternal. The results are not temporary and fading. The souls brought into the kingdom are gathered unto the final and glorious harvest day of the whole creation. Sower and reaper shall share a common immortality. They shall rejoice together in the immortal fruits. Hence there shall be the reaper's reward in the present, and joy with the Sower hereafter when He shall "see of the travail of His soul, and be satisfied."

But the Master remembers that the sower's pain must precede the reaper's perfect joy. "Herein," He says, with a touch of sadness in His tone, "is the saying verified, One soweth, and another reapeth." Though we shall rejoice together, yet through the travail of my soul the harvest shall be made ready for your reaping. "I sent you to reap that whereon ye bestowed no labour: other men laboured, and ye are entered into their labours." The other men were all those agents, patriarch, lawgiver, prophet, which

He employed from the foundation of the world to carry on His work. But He was the chief workman. The sowing was not complete until He had bathed the fields with His own blood, and planted Himself, His own body, as a seed in the furrows. The harvesting did not fairly begin until He had "risen from the dead, and become the first-fruits of them that slept."

Now the principle which runs through all these words of our Lord is full of interest: "One soweth, another reapeth." All lives are related. No age stands apart from other ages. No life can disentangle itself from obligations to the past, nor help entering into responsible relations with the future. We take up the loose ends of other men's labours, and throw them forward, to be taken up again by succeeding generations. Your life and mine are single threads in the fabric which stretches across the whole of time, from everlasting to everlasting. We are truly noble and useful only as we stand in relation to other lives. No man, or body of men, accomplishes a finished, independent work. The achievements of the present are interlaced with the past, and the same busy, invisible hand which is at work in all time will, when the workmen of to-day have passed away, weave their work into the life of the future. We live, therefore, not in breaths and years, but in those inspirations which we gather from the undying mind of other ages, and those influences which go kindling down through the coming generations and help to give each its peculiar character before God. Our bodies perish, but ourselves remain, wrought into the substance of society, and entering into active combinations whose results only the analysis of the last day can fully disclose.

But we must give more definite shape to the thoughts which the principle suggests. It reminds us of:

I. Our indebtedness to the past.

II. Our accountability to the future.

I. "One soweth, and another reapeth." This is true in every department of human attainment. Where is the profession which does not gather its treasures out of the writings and dear-bought experiences of men long dead? What, indeed, is the learning which qualifies for any profession but the studious reaping in of harvests which others have sown? The mind is enlarged, trained, quickened, and enriched by contact with the fertile genius of other ages. The taste is cultivated and latent talent inspired by acquaintance with its architectural and artistic achievements. Time would fail us to tell how largely music, poetry, philosophy, and art owe their present ripeness to impulses drawn from the old Greek and Italian masters. The peculiar culture which our scholars attain and our colleges seek to impart is gathered from the works of men who lived twenty centuries back. We talk of the nineteenth century as if it stood alone and its attainments were due exclusively to the people who live in it. It is true that in those favoured lands where liberty presides the free mind and ready skill of men have wrought grand results. But what strifes, persecutions, and blood that liberty has cost! Through the toils and tears of other men has it ripened into the peculiar heritage we glory in to-day. The real distinction of the age consists in the fact that through our increased facilities for acquiring knowledge we have entered more largely than any other into the labours of the past.

The thoughts of men who were wiser than their time, who struggled against scorn and tyranny and died unappreciated, are brought to light, honoured, and applied. The great minds of every land and age lay their treasures at our feet. Commerce, industry, politics, science, art, are rich in the harvests of thought and experience which they reap from the toils of centuries. Our boasted civilisation is the fruit of conflict, pain, and sacrifice. Ay, its best elements have sprung from the cross of the despised Nazarene, the man Christ Jesus.

These hasty suggestions disclose to us what may be called a law of "vicarious suffering," wrought into the constitution of human society. The world's best gifts have been enjoyed by those who did not labour for them. Their authors, discoverers, or inventors more often died in poverty and exile than amid glory and applause. We are taught by such examples that goodness and truth are to be loved for their own sake, and not for the praise we may win by them. To advance and establish them is the duty of the individual. He will not labour in vain. There is an immortality in which the sower shall meet the reaper, and they shall rejoice together.

Now in Christ we have the brightest example of this self-devotion to the most vital and sacred interests of mankind. He seemed to have failed when the stony sepulchre closed round Him. But out of His grave sprang new light and life for the world. Our best and truest blessings have been born of the travail of His soul in Gethsemane and on the cruel cross. The world bears witness to this fact in reckoning a new era from the date of His advent. The world's guilt was taken away by His one great sacrifice, the weary, burdensome sense of it from every soul which chose to enter into His grace by faith. The Church of God rose out of the chaos of heathenism. It gave to the world a ministry of reconciliation, sacraments of fellowship and love, and rites of holy worship. It set in motion forces which undermined and overturned the strongholds of false philosophy and degrading superstition. By an inward, silent operation through heart and mind and character, the gospel, preached and taught,—though it struggled through centuries of ignorance,—has wrought revolutions of opinion; changed our modes of thought; elevated our conceptions of virtue; altered our standards of morality; quickened our sensibilities; and opened our perceptions to the bright hopes and prospects of a life beyond the grave. It has entered into our social life; reconstructed the family relations; glorified motherhood; lifted woman out of degradation; made home a sanctuary; thrown its protecting arms around age and infirmity; and breathed the healing influence of that "charity" which "suffereth long, and is kind," through all our associations. Some one has said that "the debt of literature and art to the Bible is like the debt of vegetation to light." It has supplied the seeds of thought, the suggestive hints, the little germs, the dim conceptions, the outlines of some of the sublimest poems, or passages of poems, to be found in modern literature. It was not the fault of Christianity that the Church for long ages seemed to obstruct scientific thought. It was the inherent vitality of Christianity which burst the bonds when the time was ripe and set mind free. It has enlarged the horizon of human inquiry and opened infinite possibilities which are inclusive of all truth. It has purified art by flooding the realm of taste with new and holy conceptions of beauty. The painter has found diviner studies and loftier ideals in the story of the Christ than in the old mythologies. The musician has gathered inspiration from that story for the sublimest harmonies. Music alone could express that which was first told to the world in the song of angels. It has worked like leaven among the nations, and, fermenting in the minds of men, driven off oppression, wrought mighty reformations, overturned corrupt institutions, and made way for freedom. It was the direct inspiration of the institutions under which we live and to which we owe our greatness. If they fail, it will be because we were not worthy of them.

Every department of our modern life has thus been reached and influenced by the gospel. The joys of your home, the protections of society, the refinements which wealth brings, the sympathy and tenderness of friends, the pleasures of knowledge, the hopes and consolations which sustain you in sorrow, the consciousness of God's favour, the enjoyment of His grace, the ecstasy of hope, the communion of kindred hearts in one love—all, all have been secured to us by the living and dying of our Lord Jesus Christ. "He laboured, and we have entered into His labours."

II. Our indebtedness to the past involves an *accountability to the future.* "Other men shall enter into our labours." If we apply this thought to men collectively, our view of the age is at once widened. The age does not "live unto itself" any more than the individual. We must not judge it by itself alone. It may seem like a period of wild unsettlings, but the plough and the harrow have their work to do. We live, each one of us, in our little day. We cannot see the whole development as it is in His sight to whom "a thousand years is as one day, and one day as a thousand years." The great Husbandman is over all. The wheat and the tares must continue to grow together. There will be wheat, and there will be tares. The harvest which some future age shall reap may be better than we think. "Judge nothing before the time, until the Lord come, who will both bring to light the hidden things of darkness, and make manifest the counsels of the heart."

But there is no uncertainty about our duty as individuals. "To whomsoever much is given, of him shall much be required." Our life in the present, separated from all considerations of duty and immortality, is a bare animal existence. It becomes sublime when, by fidelity to the good and the true, we weave it into the chain of God's holy purposes and so make ourselves sharers in the glorious immortality which is pledged to them. Oh, then "it is not all of life to live, nor all of death to die." Our characters and deeds will be working, vital forces after we are gone. We shall have entered into the corporate life of humanity. But that is not all. At the great harvest day sower and reaper shall rejoice together. We can trace through the centuries of history the deathless influence of human lives, and see how their good or bad perpetuates itself. Indeed, history has no more impressive lesson for us than the lesson of its sowings and its reapings. Even we can look back and see what work there will be for the angel reapers by and by. So must the future of each one of us be. Not only will those who live after us feel our influence, but beyond them still, surveying the whole field of human action, is God, the Judge, and "He requireth that which is past."

What, then, is our present duty? The day of toil is short. The time for reaping may come quickly to an end. The sunset may be very near for more than one of us. The question, therefore, is an urgent one. To live as if we had no duty beyond the present, as if neither society nor God had any claim upon us, as if the pleasure of our own hearts were the only law to be consulted, is an awful waste of divine possibilities. It is to bury our talent in the earth, and defraud the future and ourselves of the inheritance which belongs to both. To use God's gifts as if we were their sole proprietors, to withhold good from those to whom it is due, while we waste mind and time and strength in hoarding up wealth, is to rob God and wrong our own souls. To sift greedily from our mixed inheritance of good and evil only the evil,—sensual pleasures, infidel opinions, corrupt practices, selfish maxims,—to propagate them in profane, selfish, unprincipled lives, rejecting the pure, the spiritual, and the true, is to rank ourselves with the dark enemy of God, and lay up in store against the judgment "fuel for burning."

Surely it is obvious that the part of a true man is so to live that his life may tell—"tell on ages, tell for God." The law of life is to live up to the fulness of the divinity which is in us, and not merely to be. Our first duty is to make our own characters fruitful. We can only do this by opening our hearts to the power of the Christ and suffering His sharp truth to plough through our pride and break up our fallow ground. We can only do this by entering into the sonship which He has manifested and made possible for us. We can only do this by listening to the voice of God dwelling in us, and walking worthy of Him, in all purity and goodness and truth.

Living thus in trustful surrender to the love and power of Jesus Christ, we shall have our fruit unto holiness. Our personal, though unconscious, influence will be for good: and not only so; every impulse of our hearts will be to make the world better and brighter and happier for our living. It is certainly a truth, and one alike to encourage and warn, that the grave will not end our influence in time. We hold within ourselves forces and influences which work upon our children and our friends, and through them upon society, and will be reproducing themselves, for good or for bad, long after we are gone. Some of us may be thinking that our course in life, if it be selfish and for evil, concerns only ourselves personally; but "no man liveth unto himself, and no man dieth unto himself." When the great harvest day shall come, sower and reaper shall meet in the presence of the Lord of the harvest. Then, if we have lived only for ourselves, we shall have to meet the doom of unprofitable servants; or, worse than profitless, we may find ourselves responsible for whole harvests of tares which we by our evil lives sowed in God's field. It is said that there are whole pages in the Domesday-book of England upon which is written the word, "Waste, waste, waste." They tell the story of the vindictive invasion of William the Conqueror. How many lives are like that in the sight of God! Whole pages of days and years which tell one story of waste—waste of talent, time, manhood, opportunity, influence, and of the divine forbearance.

But if you choose the good, the right, the true, the pure, you will be sowing ever-flowering influences which shall bear their harvests of blessing long after you have gone. The angel reapers may bring ripe sheaves at the last and call them yours, which you scarce dare to own. Your life, which may seem at the close of its brief day so profitless, showing little more in the retrospect than the daily round, the common task, may be found rich in fruits which ripened long years after the sun had set for you. Then sower and reaper shall rejoice together! You may have gone forth " weeping, bearing precious seed "; then you shall " come again with joy, bringing your sheaves with you."

XV.

Reality in the Christian Life.

XV.

REALITY IN THE CHRISTIAN LIFE.

Not every one that saith unto me, Lord, Lord, shall enter into the kingdom of heaven; but he that doeth the will of my Father which is in heaven.—ST. MATT. vii. 21.

I WISH that Christian people realised more vividly than they do that the most unanswerable argument for Christianity is a Christian life. This is the sort of demonstration which the world needs to-day. When the telegraphic wires fail to transmit a message, men do not pronounce the whole telegraphic system a fraud; they know that there is some break in the lines or derangement of the batteries. When Christianity fails to appear in the lives of those who are called Christians, the world is ready to say the whole thing is false. This is unreasonable, but it illustrates our responsibility as professors of religion. If we expect Christianity to prevail, we must show that it is a power. We are the lines along which the power may and ought to move. If the power seems to fail, it is not because there is no power, but because there is a break in the lines which should transmit the power. Now, I propose to speak of reality in the Christian life. Our Lord sets it forth in the text, contrasting it with the mere form or appearance of religion. He says that no one shall enter into the kingdom of heaven who does not do something more real than call Him " Lord, Lord!" The test of reality is doing the will of His Father which is in heaven. No professions, forms, words, feelings, are real without this. I do not forget that Christianity must have its outward forms and expressions. He does not condemn these. "With the heart man believeth unto righteousness; and with the mouth confession is made unto salvation." But the outward forms are nothing if they are not the expressions of a living, moving, controlling principle. I like that word "real." It means something which is sound through and through. It means something which is not afraid to face the light; something which is not afraid to be sifted; something which is what it seems to be. Men in these days are rightly impatient of shams. They look sharply into things, and they detect shams in others, even though they may be counterfeit themselves. They expect practice to be plumb with professions. They generally respect consistency, and know it when they see it. What might not the Christian Church do, in every community where it is planted, if all the influence, wealth, talent, and energy which are nominally on its side were really Christian— that is, really consecrated? It is startling to think that, not being so, many must be of those of whom the Saviour says, "They shall not enter the kingdom of heaven." Outside of it now, they are in danger of being left in the outer darkness when the Bridegroom comes. But we will pass directly to the point of our Saviour's words. "To do God's will" is the test or measure of reality in the Christian life.

I. And first let us bring to the test *our professions of faith*. Of course, professions are false if the faith professed is not genuine. Obedience is essential to the genuineness of faith.

There is nothing contradictory to the doctrine, "By grace are ye saved, through faith," in our Lord's requirement of obedience. He tells us, as you remember, in another place, "This is the will of God, that ye believe on Him whom He hath sent." But faith is the purest form of obedience. It is not the mere assent of the intellect to the truth about Christ. It is the surrender of the whole man to Him. It involves the giving up of the will to His rule. Nothing less than this can satisfy the demands of the gospel, or avail to save our souls. We come to Christ to be saved from sin. His atoning blood is the pledge of pardon to those who believe; but we cannot honestly believe that we are pardoned if in the determined purpose of our soul we are not at war with the sin which crucified Him. We realise the assurance of pardon, in the dawning of a new life, by working with Christ to overcome sin and be righteous. This is our repentance. The man who really submits to the power of the cross is ever repenting—not merely feeling self-condemned and sorry, but ever turning with a steady will from darkness to light. So faith works; and, working repentance, must there not be a very real obedience in it? Is not the constant crucifixion of self and the world a very real thing? Do you profess to believe, and have there not been times in your experience when Christ's will seemed to cross your dearest inclinations; when His promises seemed vague and distant compared with the present delights which the world offers; when some easy, flowery course of sin has opened before you, and made His way look hard and uninviting, or the scruples and perplexities and self-denials of His service made the yoke chafe so that you have almost been tempted to throw it off? To take the hard and uninviting way when we reach these cross-roads of temptation, to let the present delights go and venture all upon the vague and distant promises, to nail the inclinations and thoughts and passions to the cross when they oppose His will, to bear the yoke manfully when it chafes, remembering who fainted and died under the burden of our guilt—this is the work of a real faith. They do err who suppose that faith is a cold assent to certain truths, or a mere emotion. The further a true believer travels on in a

Christian life, the more keenly does he realise that to walk by faith involves duties and conflicts and self-denials. If the faith which you profess does not bring your thoughts into captivity to the obedience of Christ, and overcome your lusts, and repel your temptations, and make you honest and true and useful in your daily life, it is not Christ's fault. Your faith is not real. You do not want to be saved. You may want and hope to be saved from eternal punishment hereafter, but you do not want to be saved from sin now. If you did, you would have but one controlling purpose in life, namely, to do God's will, whenever it may speak in your consciences, and wherever it may lead, or whatever it may cost.

But faith not only works out obedience by repentance: it sets in motion that most active and inclusive of all principles—love. In turning away from sin we bring ourselves under the light and love of our Saviour. A real faith, learning more and more of Christ's sufficiency, works by love, and love is the fulfilling of the law. If a man is moved by this principle, he cannot be satisfied merely with avoiding evil and doing mechanically his duty. He will be ready to glorify Christ, to do more than he must, to give more than his tenth, to *overflow* in good words and works. The obedience which love compels cannot be measured. It imposes numberless duties, and makes them easy. It requires that you shall suffer long, and be kind, that you shall envy not, that you shall not be puffed up, nor behave yourself unseemly, that you shall not seek your own, nor be easily provoked, nor even think evil. It bubbles up like a pure spring of water breaking out in a stagnant pool, clearing away impurity, selfishness, deceit, and every mean affection. Is this obedience? Is this doing God's will? If so, there is certainly no reality in faith without it; for what says Paul himself? "If I have all faith, so as to remove mountains, but have not love, I am nothing."

II. We have applied the touchstone to our professions of faith. Let us now apply it to our worship. *Obedience is necessary to make worship real.*

Worship is the soul's expression of reverence, love, and faith towards God, in forms of praise and prayer. Our own service gives very full and beautiful expression to the spirit of worship. It calls us in the penitential sentences to approach Him humbly and penitently. It puts upon our lips the language of thorough, heart-searching confession. It declares to us, "being penitent," the message of pardon. Assuming that we are exercising a hearty repentance and true faith, it teaches us to call God "our Father." The burst of praise follows, and then the Psalms of David, sweeping all human experience, and the Word of life for hungry souls in the chapters read. Having cleansed our souls by the confession of sin, and being strengthened by the promises of His Word, we unite our petitions for the common blessings which we need. All over the land, the congregations of our people continually engage in this service. Doubtless many earnest, honest souls engage in it devoutly, and their prayers and their praises ascend as sweet incense to God. But could we pass from church to church in our cities and villages on any Lord's day, should we not be impressed by a general lack of heartiness, a dreamy listlessness, lifeless responses? Would not a stranger to it all gather the impression that it is a wearisome formality to the many? Of course I make allowance for human infirmities. He who said to the slumbering disciples, in the garden of His agony, "The spirit indeed is willing, but the flesh is weak," knoweth whereof we are made, and can have compassion on our infirmities. But the spirit of the disciples was willing. They were sincere in their purpose to watch with Him. God will, indeed, accept an honest, willing spirit in worship, even though the flesh may be weak. I fear, however, that much of our worship has not the willing spirit in it. God is not worshipped "in spirit and in truth" —that is, *in reality*. Is there any reality in confessing sins which we do not intend to forsake, in praying "Thy kingdom come. Thy will be done. . . . And forgive us our trespasses, as we forgive those who trespass against us," if we are not seeking first His kingdom and righteousness, nor submitting habitually to His will, nor forgiving those who trespass against us? Is there any reality in hearing psalms and hymns sung, and having no heart in the sentiments of prayer and praise which they express? Is there any reality in sitting where the Word of God is read, and not taking in the meaning of it? Is there any reality in praying the "good Lord to deliver us from inordinate and sinful affections, and from all the deceits of the world, the flesh, and the devil," when we mean to go right back to those deceits and continue indulging sinful affections? Is there any reality, as we come to the Lord's table, in seeming to consecrate "ourselves, our souls and bodies, to be a reasonable, holy, and living sacrifice," when perhaps we really do nothing of the sort—when we intend to please ourselves as much as ever, and hold our money as closely as before, and to serve the world no less, and the Church of Christ in its appealing interests no more? Such worship is far from being real, and if He who once purged the Temple of its profaners should suddenly come to our assemblies, what would He do? what would He say? I think something like this would burst from His lips: "Why call ye me Lord, Lord, and do not the things which I say?"

What, then, is needed to make our worship real? Is it that the clergy do not read the service well, and therefore the people are not interested? There is room for much improvement, I admit; but the true worshipper will not be hindered by the poorest reading, nor will the finest reading make the heart devout. Will a more elaborate and impressive ritual quicken our devotions? There is, no doubt, help for the sincere soul in ritual—up to a certain point; but the feelings which are excited by music and ceremonies, helpful though they may be, are no substitute for sincerity of heart. They may exist when there is no purpose to do God's will, and react in coldness towards Him. The bold words of the honest man whose blind eyes Christ opened tell us what is needed to make our worship real: "If any man be a worshipper of God, and doeth His will, him He heareth." We need the spirit to honour God in our lives as we profess to honour Him with our lips, to forsake the sins which we confess, to do the righteousness which we pray for, to take the truth which we hear into our hearts as a rule of life, to live for the kingdom which we pray may come—the spirit, in a word, of obedience. Nothing less than this can make our worship real. Being real towards God, it will be real towards men. It will mean something when they see that it makes us better and holier. They will take knowledge of us, when we come out of our churches, that God is with us of a truth. No wonder the world cavils at it when it sees that men who, professing religion, are profane or sensual or unscrupulous or mean on Saturday, are just as profane, sensual, unscrupulous, or mean on Monday. It is not that we must be perfect men in order to realise a blessing, but that in our hearts we must " will to do His will." " If I regard iniquity in my heart," said the psalmist, " the Lord will not hear me."

III. Again, we may call Christ " Lord, Lord " in a show of religious emotions and sensibilities. Far be it from me to depreciate feeling in religion, and the proper expression of it. Christianity appeals to our deepest emotions and sensibilities. Through them it reaches and subdues the hidden man of the heart, as the harp of the minstrel in the old story reached his imprisoned master and made him know that he was found and saved. When they do take hold of a man and draw him out into a real obedience, they find true and full expression in the fervour and beauty of his life. But there are people whose religion seems to begin and end in feeling. They are moved upon from without, and mistake the stir of their emotions for the whole of religion. They may have a very poor reputation for rectitude in the street, but they are satisfied to feel devotional in church or in the prayer-meeting. The effect produced upon them by music or impressive ritual is supposed by some of this class to be true devotion, though it yields nothing of change or reformation in the life. Balaam felt religious, doubtless, when the spirit of prophecy came upon him, and he cried: "Let me die the death of the righteous, and let my last end be like his!" But Balaam was a reprobate. Feelings which do not take hold of the conscience, and through it rule the will, are the merest flitting shadows of Christianity. A man may have them, and Christ be outside of him all the time. Not until the substance follows the shadow into the house, and feeling is transmuted into principle, and doing God's will marks the man in all his relations, is his religion real. The worth, therefore, of our feelings is proved by the obedience which proceeds from them.

In striking contrast with this emotional form of religion, we are forewarned by our Lord Himself that there may be a formalism even of good works. We may, that is, do works good and beneficial in themselves, and think we are Christians because we do them, and yet there may be no real Christianity in them. They may not be done to God at all. They may be done in actual disobedience, done with the rewards of iniquity, done to cover up or condone iniquitous practices, done to win reputation or praise, done to promote some business interest, done in self-righteousness as a substitute for that real religion of the heart which "is first pure, then peaceable, gentle, easy to be entreated, full of mercy and of good fruits." This is the point which our Lord, in the words following our text, so solemnly emphasises: "Many will say to me in that day, Lord, Lord, have we not prophesied in Thy name, and in Thy name cast out devils, and in Thy name done many wonderful works? And then will I profess unto them, I never knew you."

My brethren, I beseech you to be Christians, not in word only, but in deed and in truth. The reality of Christianity is the obedience of faith; faith which, while it calls Christ " Lord " in the public profession, really takes Him to be the Lord of the whole man. We do not call you to the hard drudgery of a slavish obedience to law, but to the free service of sons of God, through Jesus Christ. It is the Father's will that you should submit yourselves wholly to the propitiating, sympathising, sufficient, and grace-giving Saviour. Believe me, you cannot know the joy of Christian living, or experience the growth which comes by faith, or be strong in the personal experience of the power and love of Christ, until you put the rudder of your being absolutely in His hands, and submit to be ruled, in your thoughts, your words, your family, your business, and your pleasures, only by His will. You may say that my standard is too high. I answer that it is not my standard; it is Christ's standard, and the measure of reality in the Christian life. You may say that the consecration which it requires is not compatible with the business of life. I answer that you do not understand the nature of Christianity as the sanctifying spirit of a life, if you think so. It is compatible with everything in business or amusement which is just, true, pure, lovely, and of good report. If there is anything in your heart or in your daily life—any secret indulgence, any habit or practice, any neglect of duty or trifling with truth—which you know is not consistent with it, you may be sure that it is something evil. It calls for sacrifice. You must be willing to deny yourself, and cut it off, and cast it from you.

Oh, to make our Christianity real we need this more sturdy faith. Not the mere sentimentalism which expends itself in sighs and songs and raptures, nor the cold, dead orthodoxy which can only be galvanised into formal action; but a faith which has will in it, which goes out into the world with a loyal purpose, which dares to do the right and live for God, and keep under the body and bring it into subjection, and let the "things which are seen and temporal" go, for the sake of the "things unseen and eternal," and to be manly and strong and brave in devotion to the person and truth and righteousness of Jesus Christ—a faith which can say, in the strong words of Faber:

> "I worship thee, sweet will of God,
>   And all thy ways adore,
> And every day I live, I seem
>   To love thee more and more.
>
> "Thou wert the end, the blessed rule,
>   Of Jesu's toils and tears;
> Thou wert the passion of His heart
>   Those three and thirty years.
>
> "And He hath breathed into my soul
>   A special love of thee—
> A love to lose my will in His,
>   And by that loss be free.
>
> "Ill that He blesses is our good,
>   And unblest good is ill;
> And all is right that seems most wrong,
>   If it be His sweet will."

XVI.

Mortality Swallowed up of Life:
An Easter Sermon.

XVI.

MORTALITY SWALLOWED UP OF LIFE: AN EASTER SERMON.

We that are in this tabernacle do groan, being burdened: not for that we would be unclothed, but clothed upon, that mortality might be swallowed up of life.— 2 COR. v. 4.

THE word translated "tabernacle" here was in St. Paul's understanding a "tent-dwelling," and so it is better understood by us. He uses it as a figure for these bodies in which we consciously and so mysteriously live. Whether we ourselves, who are conscious of being in a body, and yet are capable of *thinking* of our bodies as if apart from them, are so bound up with them that we can have no conscious existence apart from them, is one of the questions which science in its best thinkers has never been less disposed to determine dogmatically than now. I am quite safe in saying that naturalists are no longer prepared to assert that there is no soul because they cannot "find it with the knife and weigh it in the balance." Year by year they have learned to distrust their right to pass a final judgment in this matter. They have come to perceive more clearly the truth that "they really abide in a universe," and that "the part which is really revealed to them is to the sum of the facts only as one to infinity." Gradually it has been forced upon them that "they too have to assume the intangible, if they would take any firm steps in explaining the series of facts with which they have to deal."

The fact which St. Paul states is obvious enough. We who are in this tabernacle, or body, "do groan, being burdened." We are conscious of limitations—limitations which become the more burdensome as we rise to a sense of our capabilities. Our spirits look out upon the world, and upon one another, through the purely physical medium of eyes, which we know limit our vision. We call for the aid of telescope and miscroscope to help our perceptions. Our spirits strain their powers to see further and perceive more than the bodily vision will permit. I look into your faces here to-day, and strive to convey my thoughts to your minds; but it is a clumsy process, at best. Your spirits are shut up in those bodies which alone I see. I telephone to you through the ear, and you receive impressions by sounds which we call speech. What, indeed, are all our modern inventions but devices to overcome the restrictions, the hindrances, the delays, which the body puts upon our spirits? We want to bring our bodies up to the lightning pace of our thoughts and the schemes which our thoughts originate, and so harness steam and electricity, and make the lightning-flash our messenger. Why is it, as the apostle so suggestively expresses it, that the " whole creation groaneth and travaileth in pain together until now, . . . waiting for the adoption, to wit, the redemption of the body"? Is it not because the groaning and travailing together have their origin in the limitations of the flesh or body? Are they not due to the fact that we are, in our present state of being, subject to hunger, thirst, fatigue, disease, pain, and death? All the problems which spring from the inevitable struggle of populations for existence are due to the fact that we are in the flesh, and must toil to feed and drink and be clothed. We "groan, being burdened," because we are in the flesh and in time. We dream of heaven; we aspire to something higher and better and freer; and yet we are under the dominion of the body. Multitudes are enslaved to the power of an earthly habit. Fleshly appetites and passions control them. The best of us have to confess that "the flesh lusteth against the Spirit, and the Spirit against the flesh: . . . so that we cannot do the things that we would."

Now, what is the meaning of this fact? It is variously interpreted. Some say our life is within the limitations of our bodies. We know nothing certainly outside of them. There is nothing better for us than to get all the good we may out of our physical being. "Let us eat, drink, and be merry to-day: for to-morrow we die." This reasoning is as if the embryo within the seed-shell should say, "My life is within these narrow walls; I will sink into myself, and aspire to nothing beyond"; and so the plant in embryo would die and the possibilities of a larger life outside of the seed-coating be for ever lost. Others say our life is in the spirit. The flesh is at war with the spirit. To be rid of our bodies is the ultimate good. Meanwhile the denial and mortification of the flesh is the chief duty of man. This is asceticism. We know to what a terrible extreme it has been pushed in the history of the Church, separating Christianity from the ordinary practical life, and scarcely stopping short of suicide in its self-abnegations and tortures and courting of martyrdom. This is as if the embryo should reject the nourishment and protection which the seed-shell provides, and seek to escape prematurely into the light and air.

The truth, as usual, lies between the two extremes. The seed-shell encloses and nourishes the plant life in embryo until it is ripe to break through into the upper world. "Not that we would be unclothed," writes Paul, "but clothed upon." Life in the body is but one stage of a whole process of development.

> "Let us not always say,
>   'Spite of this flesh to-day,
>   I strove, made head, gained ground, upon the whole.'

> As the bird wings and sings,
> Let us cry, 'All good things
> Are ours, nor soul helps flesh more now
> Than flesh helps soul.'"

The real meaning of the fact that we who are in this tent-dwelling "do groan, being burdened," is simply this—incompleteness. There is a larger life to come, for which we are, or may be, educated through the discipline of the present and the flesh. The consciousness which every thoughtful man has of his limitations is itself a prophecy of something higher in reserve for him. Who that thinks is not conscious of aspirations towards a state of being in which thought might flash to thought without the imperfect medium of speech, or bodies, spiritualised, move through space free of the limitations, liabilities, and needs of this mortal? The aspiration is the swelling of the germ which in due time is to burst from its environment and be that which it aspires to be. When we see a man of genius, abounding in the divinest sort of life, overflowing the limitations of his physical environment, and influencing humanity by the spirit which is in him, suddenly die, can we rationally suppose that death ends all? To believe that such a life is buried, and all its spiritual force for ever annihilated,—that it has gone out like a candle extinguished by the passing breeze,—does violence to my understanding, and is out of harmony with the observed order of phenomena in nature.

The only satisfactory interpretation of such facts is to be found in the fact of our Lord's resurrection. "He is not here; for He is risen, as He said." That perfect, divine life found its completeness and brought life and immortality to light for us through the grave and gate of death. That He should appear on the other side of the grave in a glorified form, was the natural order, the necessary completion, of such a life as He had lived among men. It was not possible that He should be holden by death. The solution of the oppressive problem of our incompleteness is found in the words which we read over our dead—words which never could have been written if Christ had not risen from the dead and become the first-fruits of them that slept: "This mortal must put on immortality, and this corruptible must put on incorruption."

But let us keep close to the apostle's thought in our text, which carries with it the whole idea of immortality, about which there is so much discussion. "Mortality is to be swallowed up of life." Life is to be realised in and through our present mortal state. The body is the school-room of the child immortal. Here, through picture-forms and the stern discipline of such preceptors as toil and pain, he may, if he will, attain "the measure of the stature of the fulness of Christ." Our Lord, in all His teaching, says little about immortality as a future inheritance, but He does bring it close to us as an endless life which may begin here and now. "He that believeth on the Son hath everlasting life: and he that believeth not the Son shall not see life." It was quite natural, quite as we habitually think, that Martha's mind should travel forward to a possible far-off future when our Lord assured her that her dead brother Lazarus should rise again. "I know that he shall rise again in the resurrection at the last day." Now, note our Lord's reply. He brings her mind back to the present. "I am the resurrection, and the life: he that believeth in me, though he were dead, yet shall he live; and whosoever liveth and believeth in me shall never die." It is not of an immortality to be gained hereafter, as a reward for good works now, that He speaks, but of resurrection and life as present experiences, making whosoever believeth in Him superior to death now and for ever. I beg you, my fellow-mortals, to think of this. Surely no interest can be more vital to every one of us than that which would make the life of the present larger, fuller, and superior to pain and sin and death. It is an entire misconception of Christianity to suppose that the blessed immortality which it promises is something which we may realise by and by, if we believe, and obey, and deny ourselves now. This idea has been an occasion of stumbling to many minds, and of much selfishness and even wrong-doing among members of the Church. "I am come that they might have life," said our Lord, "and that they might have it more abundantly." It is not, therefore, of a heaven to be won that we are to be thinking, but of a life to be lived now. Our future heaven will be the bloom and ripeness of the germ which is enclosed within this mortal here. Oh, herein is the power of a Christian life, rightly understood—that which saves it from selfishness, that which puts into it a nobler motive than merely to secure salvation from eternal torment, or to gain everlasting happiness. It is life lived up to the fulness of the sonship towards God, which Christ has revealed and made possible for us. It is life which breathes and moves by the inspiration of all that is best and purest in itself, and in God's world outside of itself. It is life lived sympathetically with all other lives, as Christ lived. It is life lived, not to gain heaven, but to make heaven for all, and so to realise the truest heaven, now and hereafter, for itself. Think how far above the low level of our average living such life, in the mere suggestion of it, is. That is a very low kind of life, we are all ready to admit, which is concerned only to eat, drink, and be clothed. I know that these are necessities, urgent necessities, with the multitude; but the anxious thought for them, which grinds down the souls of weary men and women, is just the burden which Christ came to lift by putting new hopes and motives and principles into us, inspiring us to live sympathetically, and helping us both to bear patiently and to act efficiently. It is not among those who have to toil for daily bread that we find the most unworthy living. There are men and women among the rich and educated who live habitually down under the dominion of the body and its desires—mere frivolous or so-called society people, whose whole being seems to be absorbed in thought for dress and pleasure and the happiness of the moment. In the same plane is all life which is selfish, seeking greedily and exclusively money, power, place, or fame. The man who thinks, who lives in the intellectual part of his being, who keeps himself open to truth for truth's sake, who cares more to know than to feed, who dominates the body, begins to realise the larger capabilities of his being. But even life in the intellect, exclusive of every influence which might come from the unseen, imprisoned within the hard walls of that which may be actually known, is like a plant shut up in a dark, close dungeon. Its roots may derive nourishment from the soil, but it must have light and air, or wither to death.

Faith is the opening of our spirits to the light of the knowledge of the glory of God, shining in the face of Jesus Christ. To live the Christian life is to walk in the light, as He is in the light. I mean by that, thinking and being and doing the best that is made possible for us, under all the lights which shine round us from the person and word of Jesus Christ. It is made possible for us to think the thoughts of an immortal being, alive unto God, and for whom death is only an incident, a dropping of the seed-shell that the new life may spring. It is made possible for us to overcome the tyranny of the flesh by walking in the Spirit, by keeping ourselves preoccupied with high and pure thoughts, studies, interests, and works. It is made possible for us to be in character the King's sons and the King's daughters, and to do divine work by carrying the Spirit of Christ into society, wherever we may touch it. I know that the world through which we must move is not friendly to a spiritual habit; but if we control ourselves from within, by making it a principle to "bring every thought into captivity to the obedience of Christ," we shall be always clearing ourselves of the scum which gathers at the circumference of our being, just as a pool of living water bubbling from a spring clears itself. We have the Church and its teachers and sacraments to help. We have Christ's own Word to study and enjoy, and a whole world of literature, opening to us opportunities for communion with the best minds of all ages. We have work to do for Christ in our every-day contact with the world. There is no man or woman, however obscure or hard-worked, who may not put himself or herself under conditions which shall develop the life of God in the soul—the immortal life. But we *must put ourselves under the conditions* which are essential to life. I do not pretend to understand the process by which life enters and new creates the soul which makes way for it. "The wind bloweth where it listeth, and thou hearest the sound thereof, but canst not tell whence it cometh or whither it goeth: so is every one that is born of the Spirit." I do know, however, this: that as the man who had the withered hand was told to stretch it forth, and with the effort came the strength and the healing, so by the putting forth of our feebleness, in simple dependence on His power, we may realise life. We are to begin by simply putting ourselves, as He commands, into relation with His Church, confessing Him before men, "continuing," as the early Christians did, "steadfastly in the apostles' teaching and fellowship, and in breaking of bread and in prayers." If we continue steadfastly in these things, we shall be more than mere formal members of the Church. We shall absorb their deeper meaning. We shall realise that the end of the teaching is to live out of ourselves, to help and bless the world wherever we may touch it; and we shall realise that as we live for Him, and study to know Him, and rejoice in Him, He will live in us. Oh, I have seen in the sick-room patient sufferers, wasting away, in whom mortality was visibly being swallowed up of life. I have seen the life of the Eternal shining through the walls of the tent-dwelling. I have seen the aged, bearing the infirmities of fourscore years, in whom an eternal youth was springing, and for whom death meant a mounting up with wings, as eagles. As the outward man decayed the inward man was renewed day by day. I have seen hard-working people struggle through life, bearing poverty, loss, and sorrow upon sorrow, and yet gain character, through all, which shone out in their faces and put light in their eyes— the character which is Christlikeness, which makes us meet for the inheritance of the saints in light. Death, when it comes, is for such living members of the Church only the final triumph—" Mortality swallowed up of life."

XVII.

Seeking First the Kingdom of God.

XVII.

SEEKING FIRST THE KINGDOM OF GOD.

But seek ye first the kingdom of God, and His righteousness; and all these things shall be added unto you.—St. Matt. vi. 33.

IF the consideration of what we shall eat, and what we shall drink, and wherewithal we shall be clothed could be taken out of our lives, how very empty and barren many lives would be! They would have no aims, interests, or occupations left. What would some women do if they had not dress to contrive and talk about? Take that one topic out of conversation, and who can number the tongues that would be mute, or the minds which, through lack of material, would have to stop working? What would a large majority of our men do if they had not money to think and plan about, or the gratification of appetite, the luxuries of the table, and other pleasures to provide for? Multitudes would be found mentally, morally, and spiritually bankrupt, their occupation gone, no resources in themselves, all the blessed possibilities of their diviner nature squandered in the service of the flesh and the world.

Now, it is this anxious, absorbing concern for the things seen which our Lord condemns. The central thought of the beautiful discourse from which we have selected the words just read is that we should "take no anxious thought for our life, what we shall eat, or what we shall drink; nor yet for the body, what we shall put on." He condemns such anxiety because it separates the heart from God, its lawful sovereign. "No man," He says, "can serve two masters." Their claims will clash, and either he will "hate the one, and love the other," or else he will "hold to the one, and despise the other." He condemns it because it is unreasonable. The life is more than meat, and the body than raiment. He who gave the higher part can certainly be trusted to care for the lower; He knows that we have need of these things. He condemns it because it is unworthy of our real dignity. "If God so clothe the grass of the field, which to-day is, and to-morrow is cast into the oven, shall He not much more clothe you?"—you who are capable of knowing Him, you who have nobler ends set before you than to bedeck and pamper the flesh, you who have immortal spirits, made to ripen in all holiness and wear the fadeless bloom of a life beyond the grave! He does not mean that we are to learn from the lilies and the birds to do nothing for ourselves. They fulfil the proper ends of their being; they realise the divine fulness by working out to ripeness the forces which are in them. We are to live up to the measure of the life which is in us. "But I say unto you" (this is the conclusion drawn from the preceding thoughts), "Seek ye first the kingdom of God, and His righteousness; and all these things shall be added unto you."

We have presented to us here an object, a duty, and a promise.

I. The *object* is described as God's kingdom and righteousness. These are really one. Righteousness is the wedding-garment which admits to the marriage supper of the King's Son. It is that which God provides, through faith in our Lord Jesus Christ. It is the righteousness of God by faith, and not self-righteousness or mere outward morality. The key-note of the Sermon on the Mount is struck in the words, "Except your righteousness shall exceed the righteousness of the scribes and Pharisees, ye shall in no case enter into the kingdom of heaven." The goodness which our Lord requires is to be developed, like the lily's beauty, from within. It is to be the natural fruit of a good tree, because, as He says, "a good tree cannot bring forth evil fruit, neither can a corrupt tree bring forth good fruit." It is to stand like a house which is built securely on a rock, and not like that equally or perhaps more showy building which fell, when the spring floods came, because it was planted on the unstable sand.

Our Lord, in this Sermon on the Mount, as in all His teaching, aimed to break up the surface morality which had congealed over bad hearts, and make the people know their need of an internal purity. The proud were maddened by His doctrine, because the faces which they saw reflected in it were the faces of hypocrites. The honest hearers did not forget what manner of men they were, but being convicted of sin they came in penitence to His feet for mercy and healing. He alone can create in us the purity which He commands us to seek. We must seek it in Him. He is made unto us, by His dying in our stead, "wisdom, and righteousness, and sanctification, and redemption." "This is the name," said the prophet, "by which He shall be called, The Lord our Righteousness." We can create for ourselves a certain kind of goodness which will pass current among men. But what of the secret deeds which we would blush to have even the world know? What of the low desires which we would indulge, if we dared? What of the hateful thoughts and feelings which only the restraints of outward decency and reputation keep within bounds? The condemnation which was written against men in the beginning specified no evil deeds. The indictment reads, "Every imagination of the thoughts of his heart was only evil continually." No man can honestly carry the lamp of truth down into the secret chambers of his soul and fail to perceive that his nature is unholy. He needs to be renewed in the spirit of his mind. I must not only avoid evil, I must abhor it. I must have a spirit in me which will recoil from the very thought or suggestion of sin. I must be in hearty sympathy with that which is good and pure and noble and true, and at war in all my tastes and dispositions with that which is earthly, sensual, devilish. I must have the mind to think, as well as to do "always those things which are right." This is the dress which admits to the kingdom of God. Society has its superficial standards, but this is God's righteousness.

It is born in us by the Holy Ghost, in and through whom Christ works upon the human heart. We get a clear conscience before God by confessing our sins and accepting the blood-bought pardon which is sealed to us by the perfect obedience, even unto death, of Jesus Christ. We have in Him reconciliation, sonship, and the spirit of adoption, whereby we cry, "Abba, Father." By living in constant communion with Him, and moving in the line of His appointments, we may ripen in character and reflect more and more His righteousness.

Here, then, is the end set before us, and the path which leads to it. It is the one thing needful, because it alone can survive to be our eternal treasure when the world has passed away. It is the kingdom of God, reared up by silent, unseen powers within you. It is in one word, character; and that, like some draped and curtained statue which the skilful artist has secretly chiselled into graceful, speaking proportions, shall stand disclosed to view in all its beauty, a monument of Christ's power for ever, when the drapery of the flesh has fallen off and the fashion of this world passed away.

II. Our Lord urges upon us a well-defined *duty:* "Seek ye first the kingdom of God, and His righteousness." He does not mean first in the order of time merely, as if, when these matters have been attended to, we may surrender ourselves to other interests. Such a rendering of the passage would be very convenient for persons who, having once made a profession of religion, practically assume that they have no further obligations. Religion is to them a sort of insurance policy, which, having once been formally adopted, secures them, they imagine, against eternal fires without further care on their part. They look after it a little on Sunday, and perhaps say a hasty prayer at the beginning of each day; but Christ does not go with them into the common daily routine. Righteousness is a vital, all-pervading principle. It is only accomplished in us when we stand complete amid the glories of the heavenly kingdom. There is no time when it may be superseded by earthly interests.

We are not, however, to suppose, on the other hand, that our Lord means "first" in the sense of *literally putting aside all inferior concerns*. He neither requires a separatist, ascetic life, nor will He tolerate a divided service. We are not obliged to become missionaries, preachers, or hermits in order to obey his charge. It does not justify any man or woman in neglecting to provide for his or her household, nor excuse slothfulness in business, nor a coarse disregard of the customs and proprieties of social life. It is quite possible to couple "not slothful in business" with "fervent in spirit, serving the Lord." It is quite possible to carry a supreme regard for His will into all the affairs of the present; and they will be the more faithfully done in proportion to the intensity of this principle.

Precisely this our Lord meant. He meant that "the kingdom of God, and His righteousness," should be first *in authority* among the various interests which crowd into our lives. He meant that they should be the sovereign principles of thought, desire, and action. Think how many other considerations daily claim our submission, and you will understand how this rule works. We are constantly asking ourselves, in matters pertaining to business, family, and the social circle, "Will this or that scheme pay? Will it give me pleasure? Will it advance the wealth and prosperity of my children? Is it expedient? Can I afford it? Shall I get honour by it? What will people say?" Our Saviour commands us to put before all these, and determine, before we dare to take a step forward in any course or scheme of action, the single question, "*Is it right?*" The duty we owe to God is to be our first concern in the rearing of our children, the arrangement of our homes, the transaction of our business, and the determination of our friendships and our pleasures. The other questions may come in afterwards, but their relevancy must be tested by this supreme rule. It must be first, and all other interests subordinate. Happy is the man who has such a principle set like a balance-wheel in the centre of his being. There is beautiful harmony in his life. He works out results which are noble and enduring. Glorious is the religion which thus incorporates itself with our common activities and orders the whole movement of our human nature in its complex relations.

Our lives are like instruments of music. Their real powers can be interpreted only by those who know how to use them. They must be used according to certain fixed methods; otherwise they will give forth only harsh sounds, and jar discordantly with other lives. Society ought to be one mighty orchestra, each performer a master in the art, and all combining to render in rich harmonies glory to God. But men come upon the stage with their lives in their hands, and each one chooses to follow his own wild, untutored will. They are wilfully ignorant of the true art of living. They do not know how to use themselves. They play at random, without agreement, out of tune one with the other, perverting the real purpose of their lives, and consequently make a horrible din. Christ is the one great master in the art of living. When we have been taught of Him, and have learned to seek first God's kingdom and righteousness, then the rich capabilities of our being are displayed; then we know how to live; then all our powers, relations, and actions are brought into harmony with the one central idea of duty to God, and filled with one impulse —the love of God.

III. These thoughts bring us to the *promise* which our text contains: " All these things shall be added unto you." He had been speaking, you will remember, of the things which the body needs, such as food and raiment. Is it true that those who make the righteousness of God which is by faith in Jesus Christ their supreme concern in all the affairs of life have all other needful things added unto them? Our Lord does not say that they shall have a superfluity of earthly good. He does not promise that they shall roll in wealth, live in palaces, be clothed in purple and fine linen, and fare sumptuously every day. These are not *needful* things. He has in mind the lily and the birds, and His thought is that as they have all things which are essential to their development, so all things which are essential to the development of a perfect manhood shall be added unto us.

By setting righteousness before us as the chief good, we bring ourselves into the line of God's special providence concerning us. We place ourselves, in other words, where the original laws of our being may have free play and work out their best results. The body and the material world outside of us were made to serve our spiritual growth. If a man subordinates his moral nature to his physical desires, there is an overgrowth of the physical which is abnormal and which degrades him to a level with the beasts. He has missed the true end of being, and lost his soul, however much he may have gained externally. When the spiritual instincts are obeyed, all inferior things discover their proper uses, serve our best interests, and fall into their true relations. The best wealth comes by integrity and benevolence. The man who gets riches by hoarding and trickery makes his soul poor indeed; and when the day of calamity comes he has none to help. Happiness is not found by those who seek it: it follows in the path of virtue. Health is best preserved by temperance, and the secret of peace is a quiet conscience. Friendship cannot be purchased with money: it is added unto him who shows himself friendly. Honour and beauty are not wrought out of crowns and houses and fine clothes: they belong to character; they are inherited by those who seek to be and to do right. We naturally gather to ourselves all that we need for our present welfare by making righteousness supreme. We forfeit nothing which is really needful. We are able, in whatsoever state we are, to enjoy sweet contentment. We know that God is working all things together for our good. We have enough for each day's needs. We use the powers which God has given us to the best advantage. We gather, in return for our toils, the best honours, the best loves, and the best joys which the world can give.

I have said that all things which are needful for our best growth are added unto us. The best growth is that which develops the whole man — body, mind, and spirit. The scheme of Providence takes into account, therefore, the different natures, temperaments, and tendencies of men. It provides, through grace, for direct influences upon our souls. It aims to bring them under conditions which will make them most susceptible of those influences. There is a blessed purpose, therefore, in those appointments which surround some with affluence, while others have only bread enough for to-day. There is meaning in the sorrows which roll over some, wave upon wave, and the toils and conflicts through which others must struggle. Some plants need one kind of earth, and some another. Some require the shade, and others must have the sun. There are bulbs which have to be shut up in the dark until their roots have struck down deep and they have gathered strength to shoot out from the top. When they can bear the light we bring them forth, and you know how fair and fragrant are the flowers they bear. So God deals with us, in His abounding love; so would He develop that which is best in us. Few can bear the broad glare of worldly prosperity; it is not friendly to the development of the highest virtues. The grandest Christian characters have grown strong amid obscurity and gloom. Very dry places have contributed to the growth of very fruitful lives. It should content us to know that the condition in which God has placed us, whether dark or bright, congenial or painful, wealthy or straitened, is the best for us. Put forth all your energies to improve it. Seek to ripen in all goodness under it, and the issue will prove the loving purpose in it. When the many tried and sorrowful believers whose lives have been a long struggle with adversity, who have had none of this world's wealth and luxury, though much of the inner strength which roots itself in God,—when they stand forth in the light of eternity, rich will be their bloom, and rapturously will they praise God for the beauty born amid adversity, and nevermore to fade.

Oh, that we might learn that the best wealth and health and happiness are to be attained by making the righteousness which comes by faith in Jesus Christ our object in life, and entire submission to the impulses of His love our sovereign duty always! Never suppose that you can live towards earthly things, and die into heaven. Your soul is the arrow; life is the bow. The bow is bent, and the arrow is in your hand. According to your aim, so will be its destiny. A wavering, divided purpose shoots at random, and loses both worlds. If you aim at this world's good, you cannot possibly reach the glory which is far above. The world, and the world only, must be your portion. You may hit the mark you aim at, but the chances are that the fickle air will turn the arrow aside into disappointment and vexation of spirit. Where the shaft falls, there it must lie. The bow may not be drawn again. Repentings will be in vain when this critical life has spent itself. Aim towards righteousness, and God will nerve your arm with might before unknown, your life will discover its true purpose, the Holy Spirit will wing your soul straight home. But remember that the righteousness to which God calls you is not obedience to certain cold, moral precepts. It is embodied in our personal Saviour Jesus Christ. To seek righteousness is to seek Him—to let His love enter into you and inspire you. Righteousness is Christlikeness, and Christlikeness comes by letting the "light of the knowledge of the glory of God in the face of Jesus Christ shine into your hearts."

XVIII.

Cleansed in Going.

XVIII.

CLEANSED IN GOING.

And when He saw them, He said unto them, Go show yourselves unto the priests. And it came to pass, that, as they went, they were cleansed.—ST. LUKE xvii. 14.

TEN lepers met our Lord on His way to Jerusalem. Immediately the cry sprang to their lips, "Jesus, Master, have mercy on us!" They were the victims of a disease which was, as you know, a living death. Corruption seemed to anticipate the grave and make them walking sepulchres. Leprosy was the recognised symbol of sin, among the Jews, and its miserable victims were counted accursed of God, and were exiled from the society of their fellows and all the privileges of citizenship and religion.

These men were sorely in need of mercy therefore, and they found it in Him who " despiseth neither the sighing of a contrite heart, nor the desire of such as are sorrowful." But His method of dealing with them was peculiar. He did not heal by a touch; He did not say, "Be ye clean"; He did not tell them to go wash in some pool. He simply commanded them, while the leprosy was still upon them, to go and meet the requirements of the Levitical law as if they were already cleansed. They had only the assurance implied in His command to rest upon, at first. There was no experience of His power until they had begun to obey. Now, "it came to pass, that, as they went [or "in going"], they were cleansed."

That which was a parable of the death which comes by sin, to the Jews, is in our Lord's healing hands a parable of the life which comes by faith. I am quite sure that in all Christ's miracles of healing there was a spiritual meaning, because the ultimate aim of all His words and works was spirit and life. The leper represents man under sin. I will not pursue the familiar commonplace parallel. There are just two very practical points which the incident illustrates:

I. The nature of the salvation which Christ brings.

II. The method by which we may realise it.

I. "Thou shalt call His name Jesus," said the herald angel; "for He shall save His people from their sins." The salvation which Christ brings to man, therefore, is salvation from *sin*. There are not a few people in the world who seem to think that when we preach salvation we mean salvation from some possible eternity of torment to come hereafter. The general scepticism towards the old conceptions of hell and hell-fire seems, consequently, to leave no force or meaning in the gospel, or good news, of salvation; there is nothing to be saved from. But there *is* something to be saved from, which is a very real and present fact. It involves the life after death, in its possible and everlasting consequences, but it is an existing condition,—a condition as real as the leprosy which preyed upon the ten who called out to Christ for mercy.

I do not see how we can be blind to the fact that men and women are not what they are capable of being. It does seem to me that every thoughtful person must perceive that, unless some higher impulse or purpose comes into human lives, they lose themselves before our very eyes in vice and darkness and mere animalism. It is not by summing up the open acts of wrong or crime that we prove men the victims of a spiritual leprosy. The average man or woman is not criminal or even vicious. It is easy to gather up the daily records of the police-courts and argue that all men would be bad if they dared. There are good and kind deeds springing up every day, among the thorns and briers and rankest overgrowth of unbelief and ignorance, which contradict any such sweeping conclusion. It is true, as we know too well, that vice gets the mastery over many, and causes deterioration and the death of all high and noble capacities. The story of childhood and youth becoming sensualised and degenerating into a low, profane, beastly manhood, and perhaps old age, is too real to need more than mention. It would not be fair, however, to say that all persons who are not avowed Christians necessarily degenerate in this way. It would simply not be true, because we know that there are thousands who ripen in mind and develop into useful, intelligent men and women, who make no profession of religion. But the fact remains that these very respectable men and women are yet under the dominion of sin. In what, then, does the sin consist?

Our Lord Jesus Christ does not specify particular sins or crimes when He charges the world with sin. He tells His disciples, just before His death, that the Comforter shall come, and that He shall convince the world of sin, of righteousness, and of judgment. "Of sin," He says, "because they believe not on me." That is the indictment. "In Him was life; and the life was the light of men." "This is the condemnation, that light is come into the world, and men loved darkness rather than light, because their deeds were evil." The sin is that men have had opened to them, in Christ, the upper world and a higher destiny than a mere temporal earthly being, and that they are so much under the power of an earthly habit that they will not rise and live up to the infinite possibilities of their being. They live up to honesty in business, perhaps, or faithfulness in the family, but they do not live up to God. Spiritually they may be in darkness or slow decline. The leprosy which has seized upon humanity, and become a living, encroaching death, appears in the fact that men make darkness their element, that they even deny their capacity for a spiritual and immortal life, and that they choose to live "without hope and without God in the world." The earthly habit persisted in, blinds the perceptions so that a man's horizon is bounded by the present and sense and self. He does not want to be saved from his present sensual and selfish gratifications, and yet there is a lingering consciousness that he has fallen beneath himself. The recklessness, the discontent, the natural religiousness of our kind prove it.

Now, Christ came to save us from this lost, this darkened, this unsatisfied condition. The language of the gospel is: "Awake, thou that sleepest, and arise from the dead, and Christ shall give thee light." He comes to restore the lost order, to bring our spirits back into the relation of sonship to the Father of our spirits, to make us know that death is but an incident of our being and that there is a larger life beyond, and to inspire a new and divine spirit in our humanity, even the spirit of brotherhood, by which He may realise a kingdom of God among men, and in the fulness of time a "new heavens and a new earth, wherein dwelleth righteousness."

II. The incident of the lepers illustrates the *method* by which we may realise the salvation which Christ makes possible for us. The salvation is a cleansing, a making pure, an inbreathing of a new and divine life. "It came to pass, that, as they went [or "in going"], they were cleansed." They could not be received back into the fellowship of Israel until they had been examined by the priests and proved clean of their leprosy. "Go show yourselves unto the priests," said our Lord. They might have answered: "But we are lepers; we must be healed first." He bids them act as those who are already cleansed—to go in that confidence, and to leave the issue with Him. They had faith enough to obey. Before they reached the appointed place of examination they were new creatures. Their flesh (as was written of

Naaman the Syrian) came again, "like unto the flesh of a little child."

Christ's method with them is a perfect illustration of His method with every earnest soul that turns to Him for life and light and healing. You look at yourselves, and think how ignorant you are, how weak, how stained with the sins of your past, how certain to break your good resolutions and come under the power of bad tempers and habits. Christ says: "Go show yourselves unto the priests." Take for granted that in the mind and purpose of God you are redeemed from sin and accepted as the children of His kingdom. Act as those who stand already purified within the gates of Jerusalem the golden. Do not trouble yourselves about the leprosy which seems still to cripple you. Leave that to the higher power which bids you go forward into a higher, nobler life. "Ye were once darkness," said Paul to the Ephesian Christians, "but are now light in the Lord: walk as children of light (for the fruit of the light is in all goodness and righteousness and truth)." Always St. Paul is urging the new Christians to rise to their privileges, and to grow by living up to and in them. They were not actually dead to their sins, and yet he bids them "reckon themselves dead indeed unto sin, but alive unto God through Jesus Christ our Lord." His constant thought is in the line of the story of the lepers, the *privilege* and the *positiveness* of the Christian life.

I think it is a great mistake to make too much of the renunciations and responsibilities which are involved in turning from the old life to the new. It is true that our Lord said: "If any man will come after me, let him deny himself, and take up his cross daily, and follow me"; but the self-denial is only the necessary giving up of our own way, the going out of our earthly, selfish habit, in order that He may have His way and lead us up to better things. He also said: "Take my yoke upon you. . . . For my yoke is easy, and my burden is light." We are like the old man in one of Dickens's stories, who had been so long accustomed to the contracted sphere of a debtors' prison that freedom bewildered him. He could not appreciate the better, broader life to which he was restored. His thoughts turned back with longing to the prison and its routine. We are like birds which have been long caged and then set free. They linger on the threshold of their cages; they do not seem to see the open door; they flutter their wings, and seem to have forgotten how to use them. It is just here that the Christian Church meets us, with its divine offices, to help and teach and strengthen us. It is the kingdom of God upon earth. The first step in the obedience of faith is with an honest purpose to identify ourselves with that kingdom in its visibility by a public confession of our faith in baptism and confirmation. The first Christians (taught by the apostles of our Lord Himself), in the freshness of their Heaven-inspired wisdom, were baptised, and then, we are told, "they continued steadfastly in the apostles' teaching and fellowship, and in the breaking of bread and the prayers." These are our privileges. We are brought at once into relation with an order of Christ's appointment, a ministry of teaching, a sacrament of love and grace, in the breaking of bread, offices of prayer and praise, fellowship with all who love our Lord Jesus in sincerity, and, working through all, the abiding presence of the Holy Ghost, the Comforter, the Lord and Giver of life.

But we are not to suppose that a mere formal membership with the visible Church is the end of our journey. We are lepers still, if we rest here. We are to go out through the sacraments, the helps, and teachings of the Church into a positive living for God. Nothing less than this can be the meaning of the confirmation prayer: "Defend, O Lord, this Thy Child with Thy heavenly grace; that he may continue Thine for ever; and daily increase in Thy Holy Spirit more and more, until he come unto Thy everlasting kingdom." He has been admitted to the kingdom on earth. The end is still before him — the "everlasting kingdom," the movement forward, a daily increase in the Holy Spirit more and more. I speak of the *positiveness* of obedience because there is so much mere negative Christian living, if it can be called living. People who call themselves Christians are satisfied with a mere trying not to do anything very wrong. They know that they must "avoid those things which are contrary to their profession," but they lose sight entirely of the other side of their duty, which is to "do all those things which are agreeable to the same." When we come to the final test of which our Lord has forewarned us, it will not be by the evil which we have done that our meetness for the everlasting kingdom shall be determined: it will be by the good which we have done, or left undone. That is a very striking picture which He draws of the surprised multitude, who had not been conscious of doing anything wrong, exclaiming: "When saw we Thee an hungered, or athirst, or naked, or in prison, and did not minister unto Thee?" "Inasmuch as ye did it not," He answers, "unto one of the least of these, ye did it not to me." They had left out of their lives that which is the soul of a true faith, that which makes it alive unto God—the positiveness of love. Love is the supreme and all-inclusive principle of Christian obedience. Not love in the mere human sense, nor love in that soft, effeminate sense in which it is often made to appear, and from which men instinctively recoil, but love as Paul defines it,—"out of a pure heart, and a good conscience, and faith unfeigned,"—love which seeks the highest good of all, my own included, in and from the inspiration caught in one great glow of light from God manifested in Jesus Christ. Such a love is not a broad smile of passive benevolence, nor a gush of general sympathy, expressing itself in sighs and epithets, but a *force*, moving for God in lines of right and purity and active effort for the welfare of mankind. It makes for light and help and brotherhood. It is like the oxygen latent in the atmosphere, whose tremendous energy we do not realise until it combines with matter at a certain temperature and bursts into flame. Love born of a real knowledge of Christ in the heart flames into zeal for right and truth and purity. It is more than the external acts, the almsgiving and good deeds, which pity might prompt. It is the habit of living the lives of our fellow-men, in our daily contact with them, sympathetically, as intimately and completely as we live our own—the habit of identifying ourselves with their conditions and interests and feelings before presuming even to think a judgment concerning them. Study the thirteenth chapter of Paul's First

Epistle to the Corinthians, absorb it into your minds and hearts and daily living, and you will " walk in love, as Christ also loved us, and gave Himself for us."

Living up to the privileges and walking in the positiveness of a true faith, you will be cleansed. You will not be overcome of evil, but you will overcome evil with good. Going out of yourselves constantly into that which is pure and useful and unselfish, the old evil habits will lose their power over you. You will be so occupied in looking forward to ever new truths and new activities and richer experiences in Christian living, that there will be no time nor place for brooding over the old life. You will learn to listen for God's voice not only outside of you, in His Church and Word, but in yourselves. He will come unto you and make His abode with you. You will keep yourselves honest and open and obedient to all the best, purest, and most spiritual impulses of your natures. These impulses press upon every man in his hidden life; but the multitude stifle them, and so quench the Holy Spirit of God.

They were cleansed. Their flesh came unto them like unto the flesh of a little child. So the Saviour's words are realised: "Except ye be converted, and become as little children, ye shall not enter into the kingdom of heaven." May it be said of us, when those who come after shall tell our story, that, "as they went, they were cleansed"!

XIX.
The Military Idea.

XIX.

THE MILITARY IDEA.[1]

The centurion answered and said, Lord, I am not worthy that Thou shouldst come under my roof: but speak the word only, and my servant shall be healed. For I am a man under authority, having soldiers under me: and I say to this man, Go, and he goeth; and to another, Come, and he cometh; and to my servant, Do this, and he doeth it.— ST. MATT. viii. 8, 9.

THIS centurion seems to have been an officer of the Roman garrison at Capernaum. The Roman army was divided into legions; each legion comprehended sixty centuries, which, as the name implies, were companies of one hundred men each. A centurion was the captain of a hundred. This was the rank, therefore, of the man whose words we ask you to consider. Though born a Gentile, he had become a convert to the Jewish faith. Dis-

[1] Sermon preached on Washington's Birthday, before First Regiment Infantry, National Guard, Philadelphia.

gusted with the miserable idolatries and low superstitions of his own people, he had turned with hope to the promises laid up with the Jews. He believed in their God, and hoped in His mercy. When the rumour of Christ's wonderful wisdom and mighty works reached him, he at once gave in the allegiance of his heart. His faith is made singularly conspicuous by the commendation which our Lord bestowed upon it: "I have not found so great faith, no, not in Israel." The occasion which called forth this strong remark was the dangerous illness of the centurion's servant. The man had probably been the companion of his toils and dangers through many years, and was very dear unto him. But as one not born in the household of Israel, he felt that he had no claim upon the Messiah. He therefore prevailed upon certain elders of Israel to intercede for him with Christ in behalf of his sick servant. When they came to Jesus they besought Him instantly, or urgently, saying that "he was worthy for whom He should do this: for he loveth our nation, and hath built us a synagogue." Our Lord went with them. But when the soldier saw Him coming, his military ideas of propriety began to assert themselves. He realised the great disparity in rank between that approaching Lord and himself. He felt that the Commander-in-chief of all the forces in heaven and earth was before him. He blamed himself for having presumed to send for his superior officer; and so anxious was he to repair the error that he sent another detachment of friends to detain Christ and say to Him, on his behalf: "Lord, trouble not Thyself: for I am not worthy that thou shouldst enter under my roof: wherefore neither thought I myself worthy to come unto Thee: but say in a word, and my servant shall be healed." Then follows the argument, drawn from his stern profession, which so fully exhibits his faith: "For I am a man under authority, having soldiers under me: and I say to this man, Go, and he goeth; and to another, Come, and he cometh; and to my servant, Do this, and he doeth it." You observe the grandeur of the thought. "If I, holding a subordinate position, myself under authority, have soldiers under me, who go and come at my word, how much more shalt Thou, the great Cæsar of the universe, command the healing forces, and by a word reach my poor servant's case!" His faith was rewarded, and the immediate restoration of his dying servant proved that he had rightly judged Christ to be the great "Captain of our salvation."

He reasoned up, you observe, from his profession as a soldier to Christ. He applied the principles of authority, obedience, and power, which he was accustomed to act upon in his own life, to the higher matters of the spiritual world. He argued that if authority was respected and obeyed among men, how much more was the authority of God entitled to respect, and able to command that which it willed. There is no legitimate trade, occupation, relation, or profession in life which will not educate us up to something higher, if we have faith to look beyond it. We were not made, like the brute beasts, to serve mere material ends, but the material forms under which we live were made to serve us. As through the visible things of the creation we reach a conception of the invisible Creator, so through the various forms and departments of human life we rise to a knowledge of the principles which are essential to our highest well-being. Domestic life contains the divine idea of God's Fatherhood, and the family is a school in which the choicest spiritual truths may be learned. Commercial life brings into play those essential principles, faith and truth; and through an experience of their fundamental worth between man and man, we are able to appreciate, if we will, their supreme importance between man and God. So military life embodies certain universal principles which are worthy of being applied to a wider circle of interests than that in which we find them illustrated.

Let us consider, then, the military idea; and I ask you, my hearers, to mark well the principles to which, as soldiers, you are committed; for if you act upon them in the lower circle of things, where the obligations are least strong and the necessity least urgent, you are convicted of folly if you fail to act upon them in the higher sphere of God and the soul.

I. You will at once admit that respect for authority is essential to the military idea. We conceive an army to be a solid engine of war, compacted of individual men, systematically adjusted, and under the absolute control of one master mind. Its whole efficiency depends upon the facility with which a multitude of men can be wheeled, moved forward, or halted, at command. Order is, therefore, the first law of an army; but there can be no order without obedience, and no obedience without law, and no law can be effective without authority to maintain it. When authority is not maintained, discipline is relaxed, confusion ensues, and the army becomes a mere mob. Yet no man feels that his liberty of action is restricted in battle by being under orders. He knows, on the contrary, that he can work out the inspiration which he feels, with the utmost efficiency, by acting strictly according to rule. He submits to law because he cannot be a good soldier otherwise. The more he loves his profession, or the cause which he seeks to honour by it, the more will he glory in being "a man under authority."

But the army is not the only department of life in which respect for authority is necessary.

There can be no order, harmony, or happiness anywhere without it. Our best interests are conserved, and the fullest manhood developed, by submission to law. The discipline of the army economises physical force—uses it to the best advantage, and secures for the individual the fullest exercise of his powers. The patriot knows that he can accomplish more for his country, if fighting must needs be, by entering the ranks, and so putting himself under law, than he could possibly achieve alone. But the organisation of physical force is among the lowest and last necessities of our social condition. Back of the army is the state. It requires a militia, as it requires police; but its nobler purpose is to conserve the social forces, to promote intelligence and industry, to drill men into honest living, and to advance the common good by demanding individual loyalty. It is no restriction of our liberty that we should be required to be good citizens. We only surrender so much of our liberty as would tend to trample upon a neighbour's rights and break down the general prosperity. In the maintenance of the common good we have the freest scope for the exercise of our individual powers. Liberty is not lawlessness, but the truest civil liberty and the best happiness of each individual grow out of respect for authority. When this breaks down, anarchy, poverty, distress, and general wretchedness ensue.

This principle has perhaps its best illustration in the family. That is the nursery of the state. If a man is not taught to respect authority there, he is very apt to develop lawlessness in all the other relations of life. But who will say that a child's truest welfare is not promoted by the discipline of the household? Who will say that it is not according to the dictates of the truest love to control his waywardness, restrain his evil tempers, enforce the laws of truth, love, and right, and subject him to the discipline of the school-room?

The principle of subjection to authority is stamped into the very constitution of things. The system of nature in which we stand holds us under laws which we cannot violate with impunity. We must respect the laws of gravitation, or get hurt, if not killed. We must respect the laws of health, or suffer and die.

The child is drilled by experience to fall into the line of nature's ordinances, if he would not fall, be burned, or make himself sick.

But all these forms of authority are simply the visible embodiments of the supreme authority which is lodged in the great God. Back of physical, civil, and social laws is the moral law which clothes them with authority and asserts itself in the Bible and in your own consciences. If we submit ourselves to military rule for the sake of physical conquests, if we conform ourselves to the civil authority for the sake of present peace and prosperity, if we obey the laws of nature to save ourselves from bodily ruin, is there not stronger reason still why we should respect the divine authority by which alone the moral foes which create all our present evils can be conquered, the joys of a life beyond the present fleeting world be secured, and the immortal soul saved from everlasting pains?

"Better," said the wise man, "is he that ruleth his own spirit than he that taketh a city." Think how profoundly true this is. The evils which break out in noisy disturbances, and which often require to be subdued by physical force, are really moral evils. "Whence come wars and fightings among you?" said St. James; "come they not even of your lusts which war in your members?" The foes which civil law seeks to restrain, and military rule to subdue, are really within us. He is, therefore, the best defender of the public peace and maintainer of the laws who respects God's authority in his own soul, who submits in unquestioning faith to Christ as the Captain of his salvation, who labours in the strength of Christ, and according to the will of Christ, to subdue his mutinous passions, control his tempers, destroy the power of sin, cast out foul thoughts, and maintain a holy character. To this, the chief business of life, we call you. The discipline which you recognise in every other department of life is absolutely essential to the prosperity of your souls. Will you honour men, and refuse to honour your Maker? Do you suppose that the God whose physical laws you dare not violate is less exact in His moral government? Believe me, if your souls are not brought into absolute subjection to

Him who has so graciously manifested Himself in Christ, defeat is certain. The state of sin in which you are is a state of mutiny, and must end in chains and darkness.

II. But we hasten to point out another element of the military idea. Self-subordination is absolutely essential. The soldier must sink his individuality in the common cause. He must submit all his movements to the will of his superior. He must go where he is sent, stand where he is put, and do what he is told, no matter how hard, dangerous, or painful, without a word of remonstrance. He must consent to be wheeled about as the cannon are. He must not carry his hands or his feet as he would, but by constant drill learn to step, run, carry, and halt with the precision of a machine. In active service he must bear exposure, endure hardship, suffer hunger, toil through painful marches, face the fiercest fire, and in countless forms subordinate himself to the cause or commander he serves. Men submit to all this from various motives. Sometimes a mere love of excitement prompts them. Sometimes the rewards of ambition attract them. Sometimes a love of country or the exigencies of some great occasion will move them. Sometimes they do it for pay, and sometimes, when there is not much risk of being called into active service, a mere love of display is the motive.

But in whatever department of the service a man may be enlisted, he cannot as a soldier have his own way. We point to the fact because it is one of many illustrations which life affords of the possibility of self-control under certain circumstances. Men will hold themselves in subjection for an earthly good, submit to all sorts of restrictions and inconveniences, and yet decline to make any sacrifices for the sake of God, righteousness, and eternal life. This is one of the strange inconsistencies of human nature. Religion is not the only thing in life which calls for self-denial and cross-bearing. There is scarcely a trade, profession, or pleasure which does not involve self-subjection in some form.

Just see how the pugilist will train himself for some brutal encounter. If a preacher should exhort him for the sake of his soul's welfare to live soberly, righteously, and godly in this present world, he would scoff at him. But for the sake of the miserable chance of bruising and battering into helplessness a fellow-man, and the small renown which that will bring, he will put himself under training, regulate his habits severely, abstain from intoxicating drinks, exercise himself according to rule, deny himself all but the plainest and most wholesome food, and measure off his hours of sleeping and waking with the utmost exactness. He will pursue this course of life for months sometimes, and all to gratify a brutal ambition.

We witness the same thing under the much higher forms of commercial life. Men must toil to get wealth. There would be no harm if they saw beyond it the kingdom of God and His righteousness, and regulated the pursuit and the use by those higher principles. But we speak of those who seek wealth for its own sake. They do it with a feverishness, intensity, and devotion worthy of a better cause. Their rest is broken, their health disregarded, their comfort sacrificed, in the mad pursuit. They practise painful economics, deny themselves needful recreation, and allow themselves no time for personal improvement, on the ground that they will settle down and enjoy life by and by. They are willing to sacrifice present pleasure for the sake of that future possibility—that golden realisation which so many dream of, but none ever reach. They will endure all sorts of disagreeable people and associations, if they see gold glittering through them. They will smile upon men whom they detest, be patient with men who abuse them, curb their tempers before men whom profanity would offend, and adapt themselves to all sorts of characters with a marvellous degree of self-command; and yet the crown, when they reach it, is a withered crown and full of thorns. The experience of multitudes assures us that it is not worth the toils and sacrifices and waste of manhood which it costs.

We need hardly remind you how men, for the sake of political place and power, will consciously degrade themselves, sacrifice their self-respect, allow themselves to be drilled into the service of some party, lay down their very manhood, and harness upon themselves a multitude of cares and humiliations. Why, if one half the thought, zeal, labour, and martyr-like self-subordination which some men display in their ambition for office were transferred to the service of Christ, they would be called mad fanatics.

Our Lord Jesus Christ does not, therefore, ask a strange thing of us when He says: "If any man will come after me, let him deny himself, take up his cross, and follow me." You will subject yourselves to drill and hardship and labour for some temporal good—some miserable, perishable thing which does not satisfy when you gain it, and must be left behind when you die. He says: "Do this for me: subordinate yourselves to my great cause; live to do my will; crucify your own desires; let not the world delude you; drill yourselves by prayer and faith and active duty into habits of obedience; 'Endure hardness, as good soldiers of Jesus Christ'; set your thoughts and hearts upon immortality; keep step with the good and true in all noble activities. The end is not uncertain: death itself shall not obstruct your march: when you stand in eternity, I, your great Captain, will greet you; I will say, 'Well done, good and faithful servants'; I will place the crown of life upon your heads; I will give you the treasures of imperishable joy; I will bring you in triumph to my Father's house, and there shall you dwell with me for ever."

When we see a well-drilled regiment marching in perfect order, each man in his place, every company moving in exact lines, every step measured, and the whole movement timed to inspiring music, we think how sublime the lives of these perfectly adjusted men would be if they were as rigidly under the command of God in their souls as they are in their bodies under the command of men. How square and solid their characters would be! How firmly their steps would be measured by duty! How, in all the spirit of their lives, they would be found keeping time to the music of Christ's love! How strong and determined would be their march against all unrighteousness and wrong! How true would they be to their marching orders, "Fighting the good fight of faith, and laying hold on eternal life"! How much more they would be worth to the world —how much stronger and nobler in themselves, as men disciplined in character, than they can be as men merely disciplined in body.

III. Enthusiasm is another and very essential element of the military idea. There must be a soul in every military organisation, or it will lack force and cohesion. The pervading spirit may be pride in the body itself, devotion to a commander, the inspiration of some great cause, or all of these combined. When that which the French call *esprit de corps* is lost, we say that the army is demoralised.

History affords many illustrations of its power. How it thrilled through Napoleon's jaded troops when he fell over into the marsh at Arcola, and the cry went up: "Forward, to save your general!" They were weary, dispirited, worn; but they forgot all, and pressed onward with one strong purpose to rescue their great chief. How beautifully it was illustrated in that young Frenchman who was found wounded upon the field, in the late German war! The surgeons of the victorious force which had struck him down came to care for the suffering. He refused to be moved. They pleaded with him, but he begged them to leave him and care for others. When they came back to him he was dead—"off duty for ever." They lifted him for burial, and then they understood why he would not have his bleeding wounds stanched. *Beneath him lay the colours of his regiment.* And I remember, too, that scene at Waterloo. An orderly dashed up to the Iron Duke, and told him that a certain brigade would be cut to pieces by the furious onsets of the French, if not immediately relieved. "Tell them to stand firm," was the reply. "But we shall perish," said the officer. "Stand firm," was the inflexible answer. "You'll find us there," rejoined the officer; and they were "found there," for every man of that gallant brigade perished at the post of duty.

Shall there be such enthusiasm for an earthly cause, and human leaders, and perishing organisations, and shall we find fault with enthusiasm when it is demanded for righteousness, Christ, and the Church of the living God? Men are not afraid of earnestness in earthly matters. Lukewarmness will not accomplish anything. A man must have a passion for literature, music, painting, money-making, or political life, if he expects to succeed. But if a man or woman is set on fire by religious convictions, and by the force of those convictions opposes wrong courses in business, goes down into dens and alleys to save souls, or away off to Africa to teach and preach, the world shrugs its shoulders and says, "Fanaticism." Those women in the West who are trying to pray down the liquor traffic may be immoderate in their zeal; but better such immoderation in a good cause than the immoderation of base appetites which justifies such crusades. We are in far more danger from too much moderation in religion than from an overflow of immoderate enthusiasm. Men can be immoderate in their tempers, their ambitions, their words, their pleasures, their appetites; but the noblest passion of all, the passion for righteousness and truth, is suffered to lie cold and dead in their bosoms.

And yet we challenge the universe to produce grander incentives to enthusiasm than the Christian life presents. It is the cause of truth against falsehood, of righteousness against sin, of eternity against time, of God against devils, of joy against woe—of all that is spiritual and distinctive of our true manhood, against that which is mean, debasing, and worthy only of brute beasts.

Its Leader—oh, who can paint His perfections! He stands before the world as transcendently and spotlessly glorious as one clothed with the sun. He was magnificent in His personal character,—even infidels admit that. He was heroic in His lifelong endurance of sorrow, loneliness, and shame. He was brilliant in all His glowing words and mighty works. He was divine in His calm submission to the cross for our sake, and in His triumphant rising from the grave, to be crowned conqueror over sin, Satan, and death! He has gone before in all the path of suffering over which His followers must tread, and He is living now at God's right hand, literally the soul and life of the company of believers. It is no mere sentiment, but a real, personal spirit, which animates His people, and proves by the help and comfort which it bestows that He is with them through all their march from grace to glory.

Do not, then, I pray you, throw away sentiment and waste enthusiasm upon objects which are mean, delusive, and unworthy of you, when Christ is before you, worthy of your most fervent love, and able to fill you with all the fulness of God.

Respect for authority, self-subordination, and enthusiasm we have conceived to be the elements of the military idea. He is the true soldier who carries them into all the relations of his life. We are called to remember, on this sacred day, one who did this. Washington, like the centurion, had faith to discern through the discipline of life the supreme authority of God. He was great in military, civil, and social life, because he was great in personal character. He was able to command, because in his moral nature he was a man under authority. He recognised God in all his private life and all his public acts. He prays, in one of his public documents, that " God would dispose us all to demean ourselves with that charity, humility, and pacific temper of mind which were the characteristics of the divine Author of our blessed religion, without an humble imitation of whose example we can never hope to be a happy nation." In accordance with this faith in revelation, he avowed himself publicly a soldier of Christ, and subordinated himself strictly to the discipline of the gospel. "He lived," said one who knew him, "by rule. His great attainments and actions resulted from certain deliberate and virtuous principles which his reason and conscience presented, and to which he steadily and immovably adhered. He was uniformly superior to the littleness of vanity and pride, of selfish ambition and avarice, of habitual vice, even in its most fashionable and seducing forms."

As he was thus under authority and subordinated to its will, his life was full of the spirit of goodness. He was zealous, not for the army or the nation merely, but for God, truth, and right.

He was a nobleman in all his relations, because he was not ashamed to be a man under divine rule, and to argue that if it was essential that he, as general or President, should command obedience, how much more essential was it that he should be in subjection to the Father of Spirits; how much more worthy of obedience was Christ, the great Captain, than any earthly leader!

We hold up then before you that which he honoured, the old blood-red standard of the cross. The Bible loves to represent the service of Christ under military figures. Paul calls his fellow-Christians "fellow-soldiers." He bids them put on the "whole armour of God." He points them to Christ going as a conqueror before them. The day must soon come for every one of us when the movements of our earthly life shall cease, the arms of our earthly warfare be laid down, the uniform of time and the flesh crumble away. The rewards of the present must perish with us. The sword of the greatest rests idly on his coffin; the flag he fought for is folded round it; his steed has no rider. But the soul goes marching on! It joins the throng which is steadily, though silently, marching into eternity. The trappings of worldly pomp, political greatness, and earthly wealth are left behind. The soul alone, in its own essential character, reaches the presence of God. If the drill and discipline of life have not developed righteousness, it is a lost soul.

XX.
Religion and Social Science.

XX.

RELIGION AND SOCIAL SCIENCE.[1]

And, behold, a certain lawyer stood up, and tempted Him, saying, Master, what shall I do to inherit eternal life? He said unto him, What is written in the law? how readest thou? And he answering said, Thou shalt love the Lord thy God with all thy heart, and with all thy soul, and with all thy strength, and with all thy mind; and thy neighbour as thyself. And He said unto him, Thou hast answered right: this do, and thou shalt live.—St. Luke x. 25–28.

I HAVE been relieved to find that others, more competent to do it than myself, have experienced difficulty in defining social science. I shall content myself with a very practical interpretation of it.

The subject, in the abstract, involves many perplexing problems. It deals with such intri-

[1] Preached before the American Social Science Association in Cincinnati.

cate relations, subtle changes, and varied phenomena that the possibility of constructing an exact science of society may be justly doubted. But it is possible, undoubtedly, to develop a deeper and wider knowledge of the principles which are essential to the welfare of society. This I understand to be the noble aim of the American Social Science Association. Social science, defined by the practical purposes of the association, is that process of thought, research, and action which seeks to discover and apply the principles which make for the good of society.

Social science cannot, therefore, be a matter of indifference to any man who knows what it is and who realises his complex relations as a social being. In the effort to evolve the one harmonious truth of society, it sweeps the whole keyboard of human interests, and touches somewhere each individual in the great aggregate. It comprehends all those conditions of vice, disease, crime, poverty, strife, suffering, and wrong which quiver through every nerve of the social organism. It seeks to answer the questions which are extorted from a suffering humanity by these conditions, to discover the hidden causes, and to apply the remedy. It is necessarily related to all those forces by which good government may be established, just laws made, crime repressed and prevented, criminals reformed, public morality advanced, and sound principles of economy, trade, and finance diffused. Surely a science so wide in its scope, and vital to the welfare of each member of the body, can be foreign to the interests of none but the Ishmaelites of mankind.

I am to speak of one of the forces which social science recognises as a necessary factor in the problem of society. The subject assigned me is social science in its relations to religion.

That religion, in some form, has entered into society and exerted a powerful influence, will of course be admitted. It is a fact of history, and needs no proof.

That it is a necessary social element we may also safely assume. The least partial students of social science admit this. Says Herbert Spencer: "However dominant may become the moral sentiment enlisted in behalf of humanity, it can never exclude the sentiment, alone properly called religious, awakened by that which is behind humanity and behind all other things. A religious system is a normal and essential factor in every evolving society. The specialties of it have certain fitnesses to the social conditions. While its form is temporary, its substance is permanent. Physical science also, in crowding out the old faith, recognises the need of some religion by offering its cosmic emotions as a substitute."

But we may go a step further, and assume also that the religion which has entered into and baptised our civilisation with the name of its founder, Christ, has claims upon social science which no other religion presents. You will not expect me to enter upon a comparison of religions to prove this. There can be no question of precedence in authority between it and the systems of Sakya-muni, Confucius, Zoroaster, or Mohammed. We may recognise in these many germs of the truth. We admit that Judaism is the stock out of which it grew. But there is no rivalry between these systems and Christianity. It has an acknowledged superiority, which can only be contested by some of those products of modern thought which propose to supersede it. None of them, however, have attained sufficient ripeness to be treated otherwise than incidentally in their relations to the religion of Christ.

We shall take it for granted, therefore, that by the term "religion," in the question before us, the Christian religion is meant.

What has social science to do with it, or, in other words, what has the eager, prying thought of the age, which seeks to evolve order out of social chaos, to do with the "true light, which lighteth every man that cometh into the world"?

We claim that Christianity is related to social science in the fact that it discloses principles and sets in motion forces which are vital to the interests of society in all its departments.

We do not claim that it supplies rules which apply to every specific relation of our social life. We should entirely miss its distinctive character if we applied it in this way. Rules are the outgrowth of principles, and may be modified by circumstances. Christianity embodies the unchanging principles. It contains the first truths of society, which are as inseparable from its growth and perfection as an organic whole as the silent influences outstreaming from the sun are inseparable from the development of the kingdom of nature.

Now, in order to demonstrate this, we must show what the religion of the Bible essentially is.

The portion of Scripture just read discloses the essence of it. The certain lawyer who stood up and tempted Christ, saying, "What shall I do to inherit eternal life?" gave expression to the need which religion meets. He was referred back to the law of which he was a teacher. "What is written in the law?" said Christ, "how readest thou?" He answered: "Thou shalt love the Lord thy God with all thy heart, and soul, and mind, and strength; and thy neighbour as thyself." Our Lord declared that he had answered right. "Do this," He added, "and thou shalt live."

Now, it is at just this point of doing that the relations of Christianity to Judaism appear. It is true that the lawyer stated that which was the essence of religion under the law, but Christ assented to it as the necessary condition of eternal life under the gospel. He introduced no new law. He expressly said that He came not to destroy, but to fulfil. The grand end of His mission was not to create a new religion, but to realise the old in the new life which He created. The love which a stern "thou shalt" could not compel, He warmed into being by the manifestation of God's constraining love. He transferred the sanctions of law from Sinai to Calvary. The faith which He requires is a faith which works by love—a faith which Paul declares to be nothing without charity, a faith which proves itself by loyalty to Christ; and "This," He says, "is my commandment, that ye love one another, as I have loved you." It was a new commandment in the measure and motive of it—"as I have loved you"; but in principle it was, as John tells his disciples, the "old commandment which ye have heard from the beginning." Because "love is the fulfilling of the law," Christianity exalts charity, or love, above all other virtues.

The essence of religion, therefore, is the same under the gospel as under the law. But Christianity, as distinguished from Judaism, is that truth embodied in Jesus Christ which establishes man in relations of love to God and his fellow-men.

In reaching this definition of religion we gain an important point, for we prove that it is superior to those distortions of it which are so commonly confounded with it; we separate it from the miscomprehensions and perversions which human ignorance or prejudice has fastened upon it; we refute the assertion that its "ideal is negative rather than positive, passive rather than active, innocence rather than nobleness, abstinence from evil rather than energetic pursuit of good"; we see that it is more than its institutions, its theologies, and its rituals. These may be defective, and change their forms from age to age; but religion works through them to ripeness, as the grain of mustard-seed to which it is likened develops through slow processes into a great tree, or a little leaven leavens gradually the whole lump.

We are to show that religion in this sense is vital to the interests of society. The law, "Thou shalt love the Lord thy God with all thy heart, and soul, and mind, and strength; and thy neighbour as thyself," regards man in a threefold relation—to himself, to his neighbour, and to his God. The principles of Christianity are really contained in the one law of love, which is to govern these relations.

The duties which belong to man in his relations to himself and to his neighbours constitute morality. No one presumes to doubt that morality is vital to the welfare of society. All science—physical, metaphysical, and social—bears witness to its sacred and supreme importance. All serious scientific thinkers are quick to repudiate an immoral tendency in their teaching. Systems which conflict with Christianity, and ignore immortality and a personal God, are foremost to claim a moral good as their logical outcome.

It is clear that under the head of man's relations to himself and to his neighbour all possible social questions are included. It is the work of social science to discover the obligations which belong to those relations. Social science is, therefore, inseparably rooted in morality. Now, in the precept, "Thou shalt love thy neighbour as thyself," we have a moral principle of fundamental and unchanging importance. This is so manifest that the best of our sceptical philosophers agree to approve it. John Stuart Mill classes it with those noble moralities of which he says it is impossible "that they should be forgotten or cease to be operative on the human conscience while human beings remain cultivated or civilised." Comte, the philosopher of the new religion of humanity, makes it the centre of his system— "the First Commandment, to which there is no second." We are aware that they do not credit it to Christianity, that they are very careful to show that it originated in the ancient philosophies, and to displace it from its religious sanctions.

It is sufficient, however, for our present purpose that the worth of it is admitted, and that Christ has made it the centre of His moral system. It detracts nothing from the lustre of Christianity that there should have been dim prophecies of its fulness in the twilight of man's moral development. We are not jealous of the gray dawn, because it anticipates the sun.

It is something that we find in it a common denominator, accepted by sceptics and believers alike, around which they may rally, and from which they may work out, theoretically at least, the problems of society.

We claim that to love your neighbour as yourself is not only an excellent principle, but that it is in itself a perfect and inclusive morality.

The love required is not a mere sentimental fondness, but regard for the good of my neighbour as for my own, involving the will and effort to secure it.

The limit of the obligation is humanity, wherever it touches or may be influenced by me. Christ answered the question, "Who is my neighbour?" in the parable of the Good Samaritan. He showed that, as the Samaritan was neighbour to the Jew, his traditional foe, so the Jew was to "go and do likewise." In the reciprocal sympathies of a common humanity, which should be stronger than the antagonisms of a race, sect, or feeling, true neighbourhood was to be found.

The principle necessarily works out the most perfect development of the individual life. I am not to love myself more than my neighbour, nor my neighbour more than myself. I am to regard society as one great self, of which myself is a part. I am to seek my own good as a necessary element in the good of the whole. If I love myself merely for the sake of myself, immediate self-gratification is the law of my life. There is no bridle upon my passions—envy, malice, lust, cruelty, injustice, treachery, avarice, asserting themselves, at the cost of every pure disposition of the soul.

But if I love myself for the sake of my neighbour, regard for his good is the limit of self-indulgence. I must curb the thoughts which would kindle evil passions. I must restrain the passions which would defame, defile, defraud, or destroy. I must keep my body in temperance, soberness, and chastity, and my tongue from evil-speaking, lying, and slandering. I must be not only harmless, but a useful member of society, developing all my powers. I must be as careful to preserve health, in order that I may neither be a burden nor transmit disease, as I am to preserve character, in order that my influence may be wholesome.

The law of love, therefore, puts self where it

belongs. It does not involve entire self-abnegation, as some have claimed. It perfectly reconciles the principles of egoism and altruism, as Spencer calls them, or, to use more familiar terms, "self-love and love for others." These are not contradictory principles. Self and others find their essential unity in the one inclusive law of love, as the planets, moving in their separate orbits, are parts of a majestic system, and roll on without jarring, in perfect order, under the one harmonising law of gravitation. Legitimate self-love is simply love governing self or the individual in the interests of society. I am a unit of the great aggregate. Social science says the character of the aggregate is determined by the character of the units. The law of love is the true social principle, which requires that the units shall live, not for self and others, not for self in others, but for self for the sake of others. The more unselfishly we aim at the good of others, the stronger is the motive to acquire, that we may impart; to take care of ourselves, that we may be helpful to others; to cultivate our best powers, that society may reap a harvest: and to keep ourselves pure, down to the least thought which may pollute, that our influence may be good. Our own highest good comes as an incident of seeking the good of others. We miss it if we seek the good of others because it is for our good, just as we cease to breathe easily, and may even disorder the whole process of breathing, if we think of breathing. "Honesty is the best policy," but it has been said that the man is a knave who acts upon that motive.

Through each individual life the principle works out into every relation of society. Love worketh no ill to his neighbour. The man who regards the good of his fellows cannot kill, commit adultery, steal, or lie. If every man could be brought to act upon this principle, the problem of prevention and repression of crime would be effectually solved; there would be no crime.

But regard for our neighbour's good does more than merely restrain from evil-doing. It impels to the most generous fulfilment of every social duty. It necessarily enforces the obligations of husband and wife, parent and child, governor and governed, buyer and seller, employer and employed. By the operation of this law there would be a high tide of faithfulness running through and perfectly fulfilling all these relations. If faithfulness is secured in all these relations, it is easy to see that there must be purity in the relations of the sexes; that the sacredness of the marriage bond is preserved; that the family is protected; that the truest liberty and order would result from wise legislation and pure patriotism; that the channels of trade would be purged from dishonesty; and that the problem of labour and capital would be solved by a just and generous system of coöperation.

We have not, however, yet reached the limit of the operation of this law. It widens from duty into the broadest benevolence. To love my neighbour as myself is to have a living sympathy for man as man, and to care for him as I care for myself, or, in other words, to consider his wants as well as his rights. It does not require me to supply the wants of those who are able to supply their own wants. This would not be for their good. It would foster indolence and pauperism, and be a wrong to society. The law of love requires me to act upon the apostolic rule, "If any man will not work, neither shall he eat." That indiscriminate giving which gratifies an indolent compassion is no part of it. True charity seeks to know and supply the real wants of men, and not their merely superficial needs. The real want of the pauper class is help to earn their own living by honest toil. True charity, therefore, moved by a real concern for human welfare, will seek to do thorough work by reforming the vicious and indolent, restoring their self-respect, and lifting them up to the level of usefulness again.

But for those who are not able to supply their own wants—the weak, the sick, the disabled in body or in mind, the oppressed and the suffering—the law of love provides sympathy and care.

While it intensifies the claims of kinship and of friendship, it makes of equal obligation that which indeed includes them both, the claims of humanity. A beautiful virtue has grown up out of this broad obligation which we call humanity. It is the affection which corresponds to the idea of universal brotherhood. It tends to organise mankind as one great family, in which there should always be a mother's love to embrace the orphan, strong arms for the infirm to lean upon, healing ministries for the sick, strength, health, knowledge, wealth, wisdom, circulating through all the members, according to their several needs, while sympathy is everywhere the prevailing healing influence.

Is it not evident that under this law of benevolence the causes of the ills which afflict society are reached and remedied as they could not be by any external measure? Legislation may do much to repress intemperance, regulate sanitary conditions, prevent pauperism, and improve prison discipline, but it cannot touch the heart. It has in it the power of relief, but not of reform. It may reach want, but not character; and till that is reached nothing effectual or permanent is done. It is impersonal, and therefore none of the measures which it enforces can supply the force which personal charity in the warmth of its zeal exerts to help reform and elevate mankind. "There is no achievement," says a master in moral science, "like that of lifting a man sunk in vice and enchained by evil habits on to the high ground of Christian manhood, and fixing him permanently there; and the more there is of sympathy and of effort for this, the more is the character improved."

Now, I think it must be plain to all my hearers that the self-sacrifice which this law requires is not a fanatical self-annihilation, but a pure disinterestedness, which, in a generous care for the good of all, necessarily subordinates the profit, the pleasure, the care, the interests, of self. Will any one say that such self-sacrifice does not tend to promote the welfare of society? It has been argued that work, enterprise, invention, improvement, arise out of the principle that, among citizens severally having unsatisfied wants, each cares more to satisfy his own wants than the wants of others, and, therefore, unqualified altruism, in causing every man to care more to satisfy the wants of others than his own, would dissolve all existing social organisation. But to love your neighbour as yourself is not an unqualified altruism. It does not require us to care more for the interests of others than for our own, but, in caring to supply our own wants, to care equally for the wants of others. It is just because men care more to supply their own wants than the wants of others that their enterprises become monopolies, their pleasures breed corruption, their trade is disturbed by fraud, their politics disorder the state. Self-denial is the corrective of these evils. It is a necessary condition of every social reform. The clashing interests of the individual and society cannot be adjusted if the individual does not restrain himself at the point where indulgence becomes selfishness. The law of love is irreconcilable with selfishness. It neutralises it absolutely.

In neutralising selfishness it neutralises that which we call sin, for sin is essentially selfishness. If love is the fulfilling of the law, that transgression of the law which is called sin must be the opposite of love—selfishness. If sin is the element which has poisoned the fountains of society, love is the antidote which can make the bitter waters sweet. To love your neighbour as yourself, therefore, is a perfect and inclusive morality.

But we claim that this morality cannot be realised in action without religion.

To "love the Lord thy God with all thy heart, and soul, and strength, and mind" is the essence of religion. This is its first and great commandment. But to "love thy neighbour as thyself" is incorporate with it and a necessary part of it—the second commandment, which is like unto it.

Christianity *creates the force which realises the obedience which these laws demand.* It inspires the love which is the sum of our duty to God and man. "We love Him, because He first loved us." "The gospel is the revelation of God manifest in the flesh." He is brought near to us, in Jesus Christ, as our Father. By entering into human relations with us through His Son, the possibilities of a like sonship are disclosed to our prodigal humanity. He provides in the one mysterious sacrifice of Christ, completed on the cross, a reconciliation of infinite righteousness with pardoning grace, which satisfies our souls, affords a ground of peace, and clears a way of access to the throne. He opens upon those who believe in His Son a flood of light and life and love which transforms them. The darkness, spectral with ignorance and fear and guilt, is scattered, and they stand under the cloudless firmament of the divine Fatherhood. Faith is simply the unclosing of the closed eyes to God in Christ. But with the light of the knowledge of the glory of God in the face of Jesus Christ comes the spirit of life. There is a new day for the man who believes, making a new life—new in its knowledge, its relations, its obligations, and its motives. He has learned to "love the Lord his God with all his heart."

Loving God, he loves his fellow-men, because this is His commandment, that "ye love one another, as I have loved you," because the sacrifice of Christ in our human nature, and to redeem it, gives it new worth; because, under the consciousness of Fatherhood in God, a feeling of brotherhood for man is warmed into being; because, as the sculptor, stooping over a rough block of marble, said, "There is an angel in this stone, and I must get it out," so he realises that there are angelic possibilities in the rudest of mankind.

Now, if, as Herbert Spencer insists, conduct depends upon feeling, and therefore legislation, education, and the mere inculcation of moral precepts are powerless to work moral reforms, surely religion supplies in the feeling which it excites a moral force of the first importance to society. Can there be a higher feeling than the love of God which it inspires? Must it not produce the highest kind of character and of action? There may be, of course, a certain kind of moral action without religion. Men may be kept in the grooves of moral duty by the pressure of fear, self-interest, custom, or public sentiment. But there is no "living spirit in the wheels." The true morality which proceeds from a principle of love to our neighbour, and is a governing, unifying, and regenerating social force, derives its motive power from the love of God.

It is a matter of fact that the uniform tendency of Christianity has been to produce such a morality. This appears in its singularly aggressive character. It has kindled in its disciples a burning enthusiasm for humanity; it has made them eager to do good to their fellow-men; it has reached and leavened, through their efforts, whole nations.

It appears also in the personal graces of humility, meekness, patience, forgiveness, truth, and charity, which are peculiarly its own; in the sanctity which it has given to human life; in the honour which it has restored to woman; in the sacredness which it has attached to the marriage bond; in the place which it has given to the family as the true unit of society; in the beautiful home life which has sprung up in its path; in the gradual abolition of slavery; in diminishing the atrocity of wars, and in developing the unity of nations.

We know that these effects have been produced through strife, revolution, and blood. It could not be otherwise, progressing, as Christianity has done, through human infirmity, ignorance, and sin. But the fact remains that it is everywhere associated with the best fruits of social progress and the highest and purest civilisation.

The argument is strengthened by another

fact, which is an undeniable fact of history, viz., that the law of love was not a regenerating social force before the dawn of Christianity.

It is true that Cicero maintained the doctrine of universal brotherhood as distinctly as it was afterwards maintained by the Christian Church; that Lucan expatiated with all the fervour of a Christian poet upon " the time when the human race will cast aside its weapons and all nations learn to love"; that Seneca anticipated the highest Christian duty when he said: " The duty of a citizen is in nothing to consider his own interests distinct from that of others, as the hand or foot, if they possessed reason and understood the law of nature, would do, and wish nothing that had not some relation to the rest of the body"; that Marcus Aurelius, in meditations (not derived from Christianity), embodied the purest moral sentiments.

It is true that Judaism contains the law of love, and that the ethics of Christianity were reflected in scattered fragments, as in a broken mirror, through all the ethnic religions.

But it is also true that the moral ideas which lay like the dry bones in Ezekiel's vision upon the surface of the ancient world, some of them jointed into systems of religion and philosophy, did not become instinct with life and rise up, a mighty living host, until Christ came and breathed upon them the breath of God. He did not merely utter pure sentiments: He realised them in His own spotless character and holy life. He gave to the world, in Himself, the inspiration of a great moral ideal. "In Him was life, and the life was the light of men."

The testimony of Lecky is valuable in this connection, because he is no partial witness for Christianity. He displays the broad chasm that existed between the Roman moralists and the Roman people. "On the one hand," he says, "we find a system of ethics of which, when we consider the range and beauty of its prospects, the sublimity of the motives to which it appealed, and its perfect freedom from superstitious elements, it is not too much to say that, though it may have been equalled, it has never been surpassed. On the other hand, we find a society almost destitute of moralising institutions, occupations, or beliefs, existing under an economical and political system which inevitably led to general depravity, and passionately addicted to the most brutalising amusements. The moral code, while it expanded in theoretical catholicity, had contracted in practical applications." He shows that the regenerating power of Christianity, contrasted with a beautiful but lifeless philosophy, resided in the fact that it united with its distinctive teaching a pure and noble system of ethics, which it proved itself capable of realising in action.

Now, John Stuart Mill finds fault with religion because it tends to stereotype morality, and may, therefore, seem to give divine sanctions to false principles. But he admits that to love your neighbour as yourself is a noble morality, which society can never outgrow and remain civilised. It is the distinctive glory of Christianity that it *has* stereotyped this principle as its own all-inclusive morality, and enforced it by divine sanctions. Is there not a strong presumptive evidence that Christianity is really of God in the fact that it has made of supreme obligation and quickened into life a principle of such universal and acknowledged fitness?

We have not time to enlarge upon the obvious

fact that in proportion as scepticism prevails morality declines.

France tried the experiment of demolishing the altars of religion, putting its profession under legal ban, and inaugurating atheism as the creed of the state. Was it a mere coincidence that during the eclipse of faith there should have been a reign of anarchy which threatened to dissolve society? "We are the only people," writes a journalist of that time, "in the world, who ever attempted to do without religion. But what is already our sad experience? Every tenth day [the Sabbath of the infidels] we are astounded by the recital of more crimes and assassinations than were committed formerly in a whole year. At the risk of speaking an obsolete language and receiving insult for response, we declare that we must cease striving to destroy the remnants of religion if we desire to prevent the entire dissolution of society."

The honest student of social science cannot be blind to the fact that where scepticism prevails in our land morality declines. We have glaring and alarming proofs of it in movements which, ignoring religion, organise class against class, relax the sanctities of marriage, strike at the foundations of our domestic life, and publicly announce "free-love" conventions in terms, as some one has well said, "which might have been translated from recovered literary memorials of Sodom."

Let Christianity, with its revelation of God, its ennobling motives, its hopes and promises, its immortality of righteousness and peace, be utterly annihilated,— let the Christ whose story has "done more to regenerate and to soften mankind than all the disquisitions of philosophers and all the exhortations of moralists" be proved a myth,— and what would remain? Would the "religion of humanity," which the noblest of our sceptical thinkers have dreamed of, prevail? It is a beautiful idea, but it has had but one living ideal, Christ, and He first inspired the thought. It might linger among the few for a time, but it could have no power over the passions and conduct of the mass. It would be as far from the people as the stoical philosophy was from the people of its time. There would be no sacredness in human life, that it should be regarded; no special worth to human nature, that it should be honoured; no sufficient motive in a posthumous influence for good to overcome the lusts of the present. "Let us eat, drink, and be merry to-day: for to-morrow we die," would be the maxim of the multitude.

We admit that there are refined thinkers in whom moral feelings and habits survive after religion has been rejected. But they survive as flowers retain fragrance and colour after they are plucked, or the tree which has been killed at the roots puts forth for a season a few green leaves; noble sentiments may remain, but moral principle, drained of its vital juices, inevitably withers into selfishness.

"Take my word for it," said Sir Robert Peel, "it is not prudent, as a rule, to trust yourself to any man who tells you that he does not believe in a God or in a future after death." This may be regarded as an extreme and unreasonable theological prejudice. But place by the side of it the sentiment of a zealous servant of science, who told Agassiz that the "age of real civilisation would have begun when you could go out and shoot a man for scientific purposes." The contrast proves that the statesman was not so very unreasonable, after all.

We will as briefly as possible sum up our argument. To love your neighbour as yourself is a perfect and inclusive morality; but this morality cannot be realised in action apart from the Christian religion, which gives it force and vitality. Christianity, therefore, which incorporates our duty to man with our duty to God, and inspires the love which fulfils them, contains the principles and forces which are fundamentally essential to the welfare of society.

It follows that the question of social science, in its relation to religion, is not a question of the utility of religion, but of the first truths of social science itself. Christianity, as your honoured secretary has well expressed it, is the cherishing seed-bed and nursery of social science. We call it a new science, but it originated with Jesus Christ. I once thought that I had composed a tune; but after several months I found the identical melody, just as I had written it, in an old music-book. My composition was only a memory. Our social science has its original in the principles which Christ affirmed nineteen centuries ago—the principles of humanity, and universal brotherhood, and eternal right. The wave of harmony which He set in motion has struck our thought, and formulates itself in new methods of social reform. It was the central idea of His mission to new create the human race and restore it to God in the unity of a spiritual kingdom. No such thought as this, or nearly proximate to this, had ever before been taken up by any living character in history. It was a conception not limited to His own nation, but including all races of men, and covering in its evolution the whole of time. Social science, to work out the truth, must see in Him its master.

It is a sign of no little cheer, when the air is full of bad omens, that thoughtful men from all departments of activity should come together to consider disinterestedly how the best welfare of society may be promoted.

The gospel of Jesus Christ is "a perfect law of liberty." Social science, working out honestly the problems of society, must, by the light of history and experience, find their most thorough solution in that law of love to God and man. It must, as it searches into the principles of phenomena, ultimately work back to Christ as the essential factor in a perfect civilisation.

In its practical relations to religion it must be tolerant of differences and allow for the various forms and phases through which the essential principles are progressing. It should enlist the minds and energies of Christian men. It is the special province of the churches. Your association has a John Baptist's work to do in opening up the needs and making straight in the desert a highway for the healing ministries of the gospel. It is for ministers and members of our churches to consider the practical needs of the age, and to take care that back of their creeds and rituals and various methods there be the spirit of love to the Master and love towards those for whom He died. "Though I speak with the tongues of men and of angels, and have not love, I am become as sounding brass or a tinkling cymbal."

I believe that just in proportion as we consider the needs of our fellow-men, and let love hold sway in our hearts, shall we come up out of our sectarian differences and find the common ground of essential truth. The reconciliation of differences is in work—work for the Master. It draws us to the central truth, which is love. It fulfils the royal law. Can there be nobler work for statesmen, scholars, lawyers, ministers, citizens, than to discover, exhibit, and apply the principles which work for the good of society? The principles of the gospel prove themselves true by their fitness to our need. They are the leaves of the tree of life, which are for the healing of the nations. Let us work out from them, —from the idea of Fatherhood in God, of immortality in Christ, of brotherhood under the law of love, of repentance unto life, of salvation through faith,—and we shall be co-workers in the Lord, working towards the regeneration which He has promised—a "new heavens and new earth, wherein dwelleth righteousness."

www.ingramcontent.com/pod-product-compliance
Lightning Source LLC
Chambersburg PA
CBHW030557300426
44111CB00009B/1016